PLANT-BASED COOKBOOK

5-INGREDIENTS

GARDEN of GRAPES.

First Edition: 2023

Published by Garden of Grapes.

Printed in USA

The recipes, techniques, and tips in this cookbook are intended for personal use only. The author and publisher are not responsible for any adverse effects or consequences resulting from the use of the recipes or suggestions in this book.

Library of Congress Cataloging-in-Publication Data:

First edition.
Includes index.

Manufactured in USA

Introduction

Ladies and gentlemen,

First and foremost, allow me to extend a heartfelt welcome to each and every one of you. You've embarked on a culinary journey by opening the pages of "Plant-Based 5-Ingredient: Effortless Plant-Based Cooking." It's a journey that promises a healthier you, a more vibrant you, and an unapologetic celebration of the simplicity that can make gourmet plant-based cuisine a part of your daily life.

Now, let's get to the heart of this cookbook's essence. Here, we demystify the misconception that plant-based cooking is synonymous with complexity. The five-ingredient theme is our guiding star, illuminating a path toward effortless, health-conscious, and utterly delicious meals.

So, you might wonder, what prompted this culinary adventure? It's no secret that our food choices bear a profound impact on our well-being. The author, like many of us, embarked on a journey of exploring plant-based cuisine for the sake of health, vitality, and a lighter footprint on this beautiful planet we call home. This cookbook is a result of that journey, a heartfelt attempt to share the joy of nourishing our bodies with simplicity, all while savoring every bite.

Within these pages, you'll find a treasure trove of over 100 recipes that showcase the beauty of plant-based ingredients and the magic that unfolds when they come together. It's a diverse collection, spanning breakfast, lunch, dinner, and all those delightful moments in between. From comforting soups to colorful salads, from savory mains to decadent desserts – the flavors are boundless, and the possibilities endless.

If you're a novice in the world of plant-based cuisine, fear not. This cookbook is your trusted guide, your kitchen companion on the road to healthier eating. If you're a seasoned plant-based chef, these recipes will offer a new perspective, a simpler way to relish the richness of this lifestyle.

As you turn the pages and embark on this journey, expect to be inspired by the ease and elegance of these recipes. Revel in the beauty of fresh, whole ingredients. Witness the transformation of five simple components into a symphony of flavors. Your taste buds are in for a treat, and your body will thank you for the wholesome goodness that these recipes bring to the table.

In the spirit of simplicity and celebration, let's dive into these plant-based delights. Embrace the culinary adventure, savor every moment, and, most importantly, enjoy the transformation that comes from choosing a healthier you.

Welcome to "Plant-Based 5-Ingredient: Effortless Plant-Based Cooking."

With gratitude and in celebration of plant-based abundance,

Garden of Grapes

Cooking Philosophy or Approach

Cooking Philosophy:

In the realm of culinary exploration, there's often a profound beauty in simplicity. It's the philosophy that underpins "Plant-Based 5-Ingredient," a culinary journey into the heart of effortlessly nourishing and wholesome cooking. This cookbook embraces the concept that great food doesn't always require a long list of ingredients or complex techniques. It invites you to partake in a culinary experience that prioritizes health, flavor, and convenience, all while staying true to the nourishing essence of plant-based cuisine.

Approach to Cooking and Food:

At the core of this cookbook lies a deep-seated respect for the ingredients themselves. It's a celebration of the abundance provided by nature, and a recognition that these gifts are often at their best when handled with simplicity and care. Each recipe within "Plant-Based 5-Ingredient" bears the fingerprint of the plant-based philosophy – a reverence for whole, natural ingredients. These dishes are a testament to the versatility and potential of such ingredients.

The approach is not only about showcasing the vibrant, wholesome flavors of plant-based foods but also about making this way of eating accessible and attainable for everyone. It's about recognizing the importance of health without compromising on taste or convenience. It's an approach that will resonate with both seasoned plant-based eaters and those taking their first steps into this world of culinary exploration.

Specific Techniques, Ingredients, or Styles:

The recipes within this cookbook are firmly rooted in the plant-based ethos, with an emphasis on using whole foods. They celebrate an array of vegetables, fruits, grains, legumes, nuts, and seeds – the building blocks of nourishing plant-based meals. The simplicity of these ingredients shines through, and each recipe pays homage to their inherent goodness.

While the recipes themselves are diverse, ranging from refreshing salads to hearty one-pot meals, they all share a common thread: the use of five or fewer ingredients. This deliberate constraint is not a limitation but an inspiration. It's a challenge to coax maximum flavor and nourishment out of a minimal ingredient list, allowing the essence of each component to shine.

In the world of cooking, the "Plant-Based 5-Ingredient" cookbook stands as a beacon for those seeking healthier and simpler culinary experiences. It's a testament to the belief that in the harmonious marriage of a handful of ingredients, one can discover a wealth of flavors, textures, and healthful delights.

Tips for Successful Cooking

Plant-Based 5-Ingredient: Tips for Successful Cooking

Hey there, fellow plant-based culinary adventurer! I'm here to help you navigate the delightful world of effortless plant-based cooking. So, grab your apron, sharpen your chef's knife, and let's dive into some tips and tricks to make your journey in the kitchen a resounding success.

1. Keep it Fresh and Seasonal:
One of the joys of plant-based cooking is the abundance of fresh produce. Whenever possible, choose seasonal ingredients. They're at their peak in flavor and nutrition. A ripe, juicy tomato in summer or a crisp apple in the fall can transform a dish. It's like nature's gift to your taste buds.

2. Knife Skills Matter:
A good knife and solid knife skills are your best friends in the kitchen. Learn how to chop, slice, and dice like a pro. Uniformly cut ingredients not only cook more evenly but also look stunning in your dishes.

3. Master the Art of Spice:
Spices are the magic wands of plant-based cuisine. They can take a simple dish and elevate it to something extraordinary. Experiment with different spices and herbs, and don't be afraid to be bold. Cumin, paprika, thyme, and coriander can transform your dishes.

4. Don't Rush the Saute:
When sautéing vegetables, resist the urge to crank up the heat to high. A moderate, steady heat allows the natural sugars to caramelize, bringing out those delicious flavors. Patience is key.

5. Balance is Everything:
A successful plant-based dish is all about balance. In terms of flavor, consider the holy trinity of taste: sweet, sour, and salty. Think about the interplay of textures too. Creamy avocado with crispy lettuce, for instance, can be divine.

6. Taste as You Go:
Don't wait until the end to season your dish. Taste as you cook, and adjust the seasonings accordingly. It's much easier to fix along the way than at the finish line.

7. Experiment and Embrace Mistakes:
Cooking is an adventure. Don't be afraid to try new things and, yes, make mistakes. Some of the world's greatest dishes were discovered by accident. Your kitchen is your laboratory, and you're the scientist of flavor.

8. Meal Prep is Your Friend:
Set yourself up for success by prepping your ingredients in advance. Wash, chop, and store veggies, grains, and legumes, so they're ready to go when you are. It makes the whole cooking process smoother.

9. Invest in Good Cookware:
A sturdy pot or a reliable skillet can be a game-changer. Good cookware distributes heat evenly, preventing hot spots and burning. It's a worthwhile investment in your culinary journey.

10. Cooking is an Act of Love:
Lastly, remember that cooking is an act of love, whether you're nourishing yourself or preparing a meal for others. Pour your heart into your dishes, and that love will shine through in the flavors.

With these tips in your apron pocket, you're well on your way to creating sensational, healthy, and plant-based dishes that will keep you coming back for seconds. Happy cooking!

Kitchen Essentials

Kitchen Essentials for Effortless Plant-Based Cooking

Ladies and gentlemen, when it comes to mastering the art of plant-based cooking with just five key ingredients, it's not just the quality of the ingredients that matters, but also the tools that you have at your disposal. In my years as a culinary explorer, I've found that having the right kitchen equipment can make all the difference between a meal that's a breeze to prepare and one that's a bit of a struggle.

Here's a handy list of kitchen essentials that you'll frequently call upon when creating the 100+ delightful recipes in this book. Consider it your culinary toolkit for a healthier, more flavorful you:

1. **Sharp Chef's Knife:** A sharp chef's knife is your trusty sidekick in the kitchen. It's essential for slicing, dicing, and chopping vegetables and fruits. Keep it well-maintained, and it will be your best friend in preparing all these mouthwatering plant-based creations.

2. **Cutting Board:** Invest in a good-quality cutting board to protect your countertops and keep your knife's edge sharp. Wooden or plastic, the choice is yours, but make sure it's easy to clean and large enough for your slicing and dicing needs.

3. **High-Speed Blender:** Whether you're whipping up smoothies, creamy soups, or decadent desserts, a high-speed blender is a game-changer. It can effortlessly transform nuts, fruits, and veggies into silky-smooth concoctions.

4. **Non-Stick Cookware:** You'll want a reliable non-stick pan or skillet to sauté, sear, and stir-fry your plant-based ingredients. It's your go-to for making these recipes with minimal oil and easy cleanup.

5. **Steamer Basket:** Steaming your veggies and grains keeps those essential nutrients locked in. A steamer basket is perfect for this, ensuring that your plant-based meals are both healthy and full of flavor.

6. Baking Sheet: For those roasting and baking moments, a good-quality baking sheet is indispensable. From crispy roasted vegetables to sweet and savory baked delights, this tool's got you covered.

7. Food Processor: A food processor can make life in the kitchen easier. From creating pestos to making energy balls, it's a versatile piece of equipment that's worth having in your arsenal.

8. Citrus Juicer: Fresh lemon, lime, or orange juice can elevate your plant-based recipes. A simple citrus juicer is an easy way to extract every last drop of zesty goodness.

9. Measuring Cups and Spoons: Precision is key, especially when you're working with a limited number of ingredients. A set of measuring cups and spoons will ensure that your recipes turn out just right.

10. Peeler and Grater: From zesting citrus fruits to creating vegetable noodles, a good peeler and grater can add texture and flavor to your plant-based dishes.

11. Oven: Many of our plant-based wonders require some quality time in the oven. So, make sure your oven is in good working condition.

Tips for Using Your Tools Effectively:

Now that you're well-acquainted with your kitchen essentials, let's talk about how to use them effectively:

- Keep Your Knife Sharp: A sharp knife is not only safer but also more effective. Invest in a quality knife sharpener or take your knives to a professional for maintenance.

- Preheat Your Non-Stick Cookware: When using non-stick cookware, allow it to preheat before adding your ingredients. This helps prevent sticking and ensures even cooking.

- Learn Your Blender's Settings: If you're using a high-speed blender, familiarize yourself with its settings and functions. It can be a versatile kitchen tool if you know how to make the most of it.

- Avoid Overfilling the Food Processor: When using a food processor, avoid overfilling it. Process in batches if necessary, so your machine can work efficiently.

- Experiment with Texture: Your grater and peeler can be used to experiment with the textures of your plant-based ingredients. A little change in texture can add a whole new dimension to your dishes.

With these kitchen essentials at your side and these tips in your culinary arsenal, you're ready to embark on an effortless journey toward a healthier you. So, sharpen those knives, preheat those skillets, and let's dive into the world of plant-based cooking like never before.

Happy cooking!

Garden of Grapes

Flavor Pairing Suggestions

Flavor Harmony Guide

In the realm of culinary artistry, few things hold as much intrigue and promise as the perfect pairing of flavors. Our "Plant-Based 5-Ingredient" cookbook is a symphony of simplicity, where minimalism dances hand in hand with deliciousness. However, we understand that you might want to take your culinary adventure a step further. That's where this Flavor Harmony Guide comes into play.

Below, we've compiled a list of complementary flavors and ingredients that, when combined, create a culinary masterpiece that is often greater than the sum of its parts. Let these suggestions inspire your inner chef and encourage you to craft your own recipes.

1. Sweet and Savory
   - Pairing: Maple syrup and Dijon mustard
   - Inspiration: Create a glaze for roasted vegetables or tofu.

2. Creamy and Tangy
   - Pairing: Coconut milk and lime juice
   - Inspiration: Make a zesty Thai-inspired curry.

3. Earthy and Bright
   - Pairing: Balsamic vinegar and fresh basil
   - Inspiration: Drizzle over roasted mushrooms or a caprese salad.

4. Nutty and Fruity
   - Pairing: Almonds and dried apricots
   - Inspiration: Blend into a luscious sauce for grain bowls.

5. Spicy and Cooling
   - Pairing: Sriracha and Greek yogurt
   - Inspiration: Craft a dipping sauce for vegetable fritters.

6. Rich and Fresh
   - Pairing: Avocado and cilantro
   - Inspiration: Mash into guacamole or spread on toast.

7. Hearty and Herbal
   - Pairing: Lentils and rosemary
   - Inspiration: Simmer for a soul-soothing soup.

8. Smoky and Citrusy
   - Pairing: Smoked paprika and orange zest
   - Inspiration: Season roasted butternut squash or sweet potatoes.
9. Comforting and Exotic
   - Pairing: Cinnamon and cardamom
   - Inspiration: Infuse your morning oatmeal or rice pudding.
10. Robust and Delicate
   - Pairing: Cumin and coriander
   - Inspiration: Spice up a simple hummus or couscous dish.

These harmonious flavor pairings are your stepping stones to culinary creativity. They are the sparks that ignite your imagination and guide you on a journey to create your own unique plant-based masterpieces. Whether you're preparing a quick weeknight dinner or a special weekend feast, these ideas will be your trusty companions.

Remember, the kitchen is your canvas, and you are the artist. Feel free to experiment, mix and match, and let your palate be your guide. Your culinary adventures are bound only by your own creativity, so let your taste buds lead the way.

Happy cooking and bon appétit!

Garden of Grapes

INDEX

Chapter 1:
Quick and Easy Breakfasts

2 slices   210   10

Avocado Toast with Cherry Tomatoes

Ingredients:

- 2 slices of sourdough bread
- 1 ripe avocado
- 1 cup cherry tomatoes
- 1 tbsp olive oil
- Salt and pepper to taste

A modern classic, this dish combines creamy avocados and ripe cherry tomatoes on toasted sourdough. Perfect for a quick and healthy breakfast.

Directions

1. Toast the sourdough slices.
2. Mash the avocado and spread it on the toast.
3. Top with halved cherry tomatoes.
4. Drizzle with olive oil and season with salt and pepper.

Fun Facts

Avocado is rich in healthy fats and potassium, making it a nutritious choice to start your day.

2
pancake
s

280

15

Banana Pancakes

These fluffy pancakes are made with ripe bananas and a hint of cinnamon. They're a sweet way to kickstart your morning.

Ingredients:

- 2 ripe bananas
- 1 cup flour
- 1 tsp baking powder
- 1/2 tsp cinnamon
- 1/2 cup milk
- 1 egg
- 2 tbsp maple syrup

Directions

1. In a bowl, mash the bananas.
2. Add flour, baking powder, and cinnamon.
3. Stir in milk, egg, and maple syrup.
4. Cook on a griddle until golden brown.

Fun Facts

Bananas in these pancakes add natural sweetness and a boost of potassium.

1 serving | 320 | 5 (overnight)

Overnight Oats with Berries

Ingredients:

- 1/2 cup rolled oats
- 1 cup milk
- 1 tbsp honey
- 1/2 cup mixed berries
- 1/4 tsp vanilla extract

Prepare your breakfast the night before with these creamy overnight oats topped with fresh berries.

Directions

1. In a jar, combine oats, milk, honey, and vanilla.
2. Refrigerate overnight.
3. Top with mixed berries before serving.

Fun Facts

Overnight oats save you time and provide a nutritious morning boost.

1 serving   380   5

Peanut Butter Banana Smoothie Bowl

Ingredients:

- 2 ripe bananas
- 2 tbsp peanut butter
- 1 cup almond milk
- 1 tbsp honey
- Toppings: granola, sliced banana, chia seeds

Dive into a satisfying smoothie bowl with the goodness of peanut butter, bananas, and a variety of toppings.

Directions

1. Blend bananas, peanut butter, almond milk, and honey.
2. Pour into a bowl.
3. Add your favorite toppings.

Fun Facts

A smoothie bowl is highly customizable; you can switch up toppings for variety.

2
servings

180

15

Spinach and Mushroom Scramble

Ingredients:

- 4 eggs
- 2 cups fresh spinach
- 1 cup sliced mushrooms
- 1/4 cup grated cheese
- Salt and pepper to taste

Scrambled eggs with sautéed spinach and mushrooms create a hearty and healthy breakfast option.

Directions

1. Sauté mushrooms and spinach until wilted.
2. Whisk eggs, pour over veggies.
3. Add cheese, salt, and pepper.
4. Scramble until set.

Fun Facts

Spinach and mushrooms provide a vitamin and protein boost to your morning.

4 slices   240   20

Vegan French Toast

Ingredients:

- 4 slices of bread
- 1 cup almond milk
- 2 tbsp flaxseed
- 1 tsp vanilla extract
- 1 tsp cinnamon
- Maple syrup for drizzling

A plant-based twist on classic French toast, using almond milk and flaxseed for a delightful, cruelty-free breakfast.

Directions

1. In a bowl, whisk almond milk, flaxseed, vanilla, and cinnamon.
2. Dip bread slices in the mixture.
3. Cook until golden.
4. Drizzle with maple syrup.

Fun Facts

This vegan version is just as delicious as traditional French toast.

2
servings

250

10
(overnig
ht)

Chia Seed Pudding with Mango

Ingredients:

- 1/2 cup chia seeds
- 2 cups almond milk
- 2 tbsp honey
- 1 tsp vanilla extract
- 1 cup diced mango

Fun Facts

Chia seeds are a superfood, packed with omega-3s and fiber.

Creamy chia seed pudding topped with sweet mango is a nutritious and convenient make-ahead breakfast.

Directions

1. In a bowl, mix chia seeds, almond milk, honey, and vanilla.
2. Refrigerate overnight.
3. Top with diced mango before serving.

12 muffins

180

25

Blueberry Muffins

Ingredients:

- 2 cups flour
- 1/2 cup sugar
- 2 tsp baking powder
- 1/2 tsp salt
- 1/2 cup butter
- 2 eggs- 1 cup milk
- 1 tsp vanilla extract
- 1 cup blueberries

These delightful blueberry muffins are a timeless classic, perfect for a quick, on-the-go breakfast or snack.

Directions

1. Preheat oven to 375°F.
2. Mix dry ingredients.
3. Add melted butter, eggs, milk, vanilla.
4. Gently fold in blueberries.
5. Bake for 20-25 minutes.

Fun Facts

Blueberries add antioxidants and a burst of flavor to these muffins.

2
burritos

320

20

Tofu and Veggie Breakfast Burritos

These hearty breakfast burritos are packed with tofu, veggies, and spices, perfect for a savory morning meal.

Ingredients:

- 1/2 block tofu, crumbled
- 1/2 cup diced bell peppers
- 1/2 cup diced onions
- 1/2 cup black beans
- 1/2 tsp turmeric
- 1/2 tsp cumin
- Salt and pepper to taste
- 2 large tortillas

Directions

1. Sauté veggies and tofu with spices.
2. Add black beans.
3. Season with salt and pepper.
4. Fill tortillas.
5. Roll and enjoy.

Fun Facts

Tofu provides a plant-based protein source for these burritos.

4 tacos   280   25

Vegan Breakfast Tacos

Ingredients:

- 1/2 block tofu, crumbled
- 1/2 tsp chili powder
- 1/2 tsp paprika
- 1/2 cup diced avocado
- 1/4 cup salsa
- 4 small tortillas

These vegan breakfast tacos are filled with spiced tofu, avocado, and salsa, creating a delightful morning fiesta.

Directions

1. Sauté tofu with spices.
2. Warm tortillas.
3. Fill with tofu, avocado, and salsa.
4. Serve and enjoy.

Fun Facts

Tofu adds a protein punch, making these tacos a hearty breakfast choice.

Chapter 2:
Simple and Savory Soups

4
servings

220

30

Creamy Tomato Soup

Ingredients:

- 2 cans (28 oz each) crushed tomatoes
- 2 cups vegetable broth
- 1 cup heavy cream
- 2 tbsp butter
- 1 onion, diced
- 2 cloves garlic, minced
- 1 tsp sugar
- Salt and pepper to taste

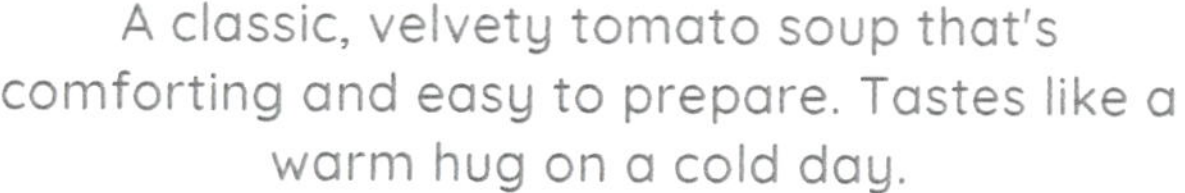

A classic, velvety tomato soup that's comforting and easy to prepare. Tastes like a warm hug on a cold day.

Directions

1. In a pot, sauté onions and garlic in butter.
2. Add crushed tomatoes, broth, and sugar.
3. Simmer for 20 minutes.
4. Blend until smooth.
5. Stir in cream.
6. Season with salt and pepper.

Fun Facts

Tomatoes are rich in lycopene, an antioxidant that's good for your heart.

6
servings

260

40

Lentil Soup

Ingredients:

- 1 cup green or brown lentils
- 1 onion, chopped
- 2 carrots, diced
- 2 cloves garlic, minced
- 1 tsp cumin
- 1 tsp coriander
- 1 tsp turmeric
- 6 cups vegetable broth
- Salt and pepper to taste

Hearty and nutritious, this lentil soup is a satisfying dish with a touch of Middle Eastern spices.

Directions

1. Sauté onions, carrots, and garlic.
2. Add lentils, spices, and broth.
3. Simmer for 30 minutes.
4. Season with salt and pepper.

Fun Facts

Lentils are packed with protein and fiber, making this soup both tasty and nutritious.

4
servings

300

45

Sweet Potato and Coconut Soup

A creamy, slightly sweet soup with the earthiness of sweet potatoes and a tropical twist from coconut milk.

Ingredients:

- 2 large sweet potatoes, peeled and diced
- 1 onion, chopped
- 2 cloves garlic, minced
- 1 can (14 oz) coconut milk
- 4 cups vegetable broth
- 2 tsp curry powder
- Salt and pepper to taste

Directions

1. Sauté onions and garlic.
2. Add sweet potatoes, curry powder, and broth.
3. Simmer until potatoes are tender.
4. Blend with coconut milk.
5. Season with salt and pepper.

Fun Facts

Sweet potatoes are high in vitamins and fiber, giving you a nutrient boost.

6
servings

230

35

Minestrone Soup

Ingredients:

- 1 cup small pasta (e.g., ditalini)
- 1 can (15 oz) cannellini beans
- 2 cups diced zucchini
- 1 cup diced carrots
- 1 cup diced celery
- 1 onion, chopped
- 2 cloves garlic, minced
- 4 cups vegetable broth
- 1 can (15 oz) diced tomatoes
- 2 tsp dried basil
- 2 tsp dried oregano
- Salt and pepper to taste

An Italian classic, this minestrone is a hearty vegetable soup with pasta and beans. Perfect for a comforting, one-pot meal.

Directions

1. Sauté onions and garlic.
2. Add zucchini, carrots, and celery.
3. Stir in broth, beans, and pasta.
4. Simmer until pasta is cooked.
5. Season with salt, pepper, basil, and oregano.

Fun Facts

Minestrone is loaded with veggies, providing vitamins and minerals in every bowl.

4
servings

180

30

Vegan Potato Leek Soup

Ingredients:

- 4 leeks, sliced
- 4 potatoes, peeled and diced
- 6 cups vegetable broth
- 2 cloves garlic, minced
- 2 tbsp olive oil
- Salt and pepper to taste

A dairy-free, velvety soup with the rich flavors of leeks and potatoes. Perfect for a cozy evening meal.

Directions

1. Sauté leeks and garlic in olive oil.
2. Add potatoes and broth.
3. Simmer until potatoes are tender.
4. Blend until smooth.
5. Season with salt and pepper.

Fun Facts

Leeks contain antioxidants and vitamins, adding a healthy twist to this soup.

6
servings

250

35

Black Bean Soup

Ingredients:

- 2 cans (15 oz each) black beans, drained and rinsed
- 1 onion, chopped
- 2 cloves garlic, minced
- 1 red bell pepper, chopped
- 1 tsp chili powder
- 1 tsp cumin
- 4 cups vegetable broth
- Salt and pepper to taste

This black bean soup is a hearty, Southwestern-inspired dish with a spicy kick, perfect for warming you up on a chilly day.

Directions

1. Sauté onions, garlic, and bell pepper.
2. Add beans, spices, and broth.
3. Simmer for 20 minutes.
4. Season with salt and pepper.

Fun Facts

Black beans are an excellent source of plant-based protein and fiber.

4
servings

260

35

Chickpea and Spinach Soup

Ingredients:

- 2 cans (15 oz each) chickpeas, drained and rinsed
- 1 onion, chopped
- 2 cloves garlic, minced
- 4 cups vegetable broth
- 1 tsp ground cumin
- 1 tsp ground coriander
- 4 cups fresh spinach
- Salt and pepper to taste

This soup combines the earthy flavor of chickpeas with the freshness of spinach for a wholesome and flavorful meal.

Directions

1. Sauté onions and garlic.
2. Add chickpeas, spices, and broth.
3. Simmer for 15 minutes.
4. Stir in spinach until wilted.
5. Season with salt and pepper.

Fun Facts

Chickpeas are a great source of protein and fiber, making this soup filling and nutritious.

4
servings

240

40

Butternut Squash Soup

Ingredients:

- 1 butternut squash, peeled and diced
- 1 onion, chopped
- 2 cloves garlic, minced
- 4 cups vegetable broth
- 1/2 tsp ground cinnamon
- 1/2 tsp ground nutmeg
- Salt and pepper to taste

A smooth and creamy soup with the natural sweetness of butternut squash and a touch of warmth from spices.

Directions

1. Sauté onions and garlic.
2. Add squash, spices, and broth.
3. Simmer until squash is tender.
4. Blend until smooth.
5. Season with salt and pepper.

Fun Facts

Butternut squash is rich in vitamin A and fiber, making this soup a nutritious choice.

4
servings

120

20

Miso Soup

A Japanese classic, miso soup is a light and flavorful broth with tofu and seaweed, perfect for a quick and soothing meal.

Ingredients:

- 4 cups water
- 4 tbsp miso paste
- 1/2 cup diced tofu
- 2 sheets nori seaweed, torn into pieces
- 2 green onions, sliced
- 1/2 cup sliced mushrooms

Directions

1. Heat water, dissolve miso paste.
2. Add tofu, seaweed, and mushrooms.
3. Simmer for 5 minutes.
4. Garnish with green onions.

Fun Facts

Miso is a fermented food that promotes gut health and provides essential nutrients.

4 servings

180

15

Vegan Gazpacho

Ingredients:

- 6 ripe tomatoes, diced
- 1 cucumber, diced
- 1 red bell pepper, diced
- 1/2 red onion, chopped
- 2 cloves garlic, minced
- 1/4 cup olive oil
- 2 tbsp red wine vinegar
- 1 tsp paprika
- Salt and pepper to taste

A chilled, Spanish-inspired soup with a medley of fresh vegetables and a zesty kick. Perfect for a refreshing summer meal.

Directions

1. Blend tomatoes, cucumber, and red bell pepper until smooth.
2. Stir in onion, garlic, olive oil, vinegar, and paprika.
3. Season with salt and pepper.
4. Chill before serving.

Fun Facts

Gazpacho is a low-calorie soup that's packed with vitamins and hydrating ingredients.

Chapter 3:
Satisfying Salads

4
servings

350

25

Mediterranean Quinoa Salad

A fresh and vibrant quinoa salad with Mediterranean flavors, including tomatoes, cucumbers, and feta cheese.

Ingredients:

- 1 cup quinoa
- 2 cups water
- 1 cup cherry tomatoes, halved
- 1 cucumber, diced
- 1/2 cup feta cheese, crumbled
- 1/4 cup Kalamata olives, pitted and sliced
- 1/4 cup red onion, finely chopped
- 1/4 cup fresh parsley, chopped
- 1/4 cup fresh mint, chopped
- 2 tbsp extra
-virgin olive oil
- 2 tbsp lemon juice
- Salt and pepper to taste

Directions

1. Rinse quinoa, cook with water.
2. Fluff and cool.
3. Combine with vegetables, feta, and olives.
4. Drizzle with olive oil and lemon juice.
5. Season with salt and pepper.
6. Garnish with fresh herbs.

Fun Facts

Quinoa is a complete protein source, making this salad a satisfying and healthy choice.

4
servings

280

15

Avocado and
Black Bean Salad

Ingredients:

- 2 avocados, diced
- 1 can (15 oz) black beans, drained and rinsed
- 1 cup corn kernels
- 1/2 red onion, finely chopped
- 1/4 cup cilantro, chopped
- 2 tbsp lime juice
- 2 tbsp olive oil
- 1 tsp cumin- Salt and pepper to taste

A zesty salad combining creamy avocado, black beans, corn, and a tangy lime dressing for a delightful Tex-Mex-inspired dish.

Directions

1. In a bowl, combine avocados, black beans, corn, and red onion.
2. Whisk together lime juice, olive oil, cumin, salt, and pepper.
3. Drizzle dressing over the salad.
4. Garnish with cilantro.

Fun Facts

Avocado provides healthy fats and creaminess to this salad, while black beans add protein.

4
servings

220

10

Caprese Salad

A classic Italian salad featuring ripe tomatoes, fresh mozzarella, basil, and a drizzle of balsamic glaze.

Ingredients:

- 4 ripe tomatoes, sliced
- 8 oz fresh mozzarella, sliced
- 1/2 cup fresh basil leaves
- 2 tbsp extra-virgin olive oil
- 2 tbsp balsamic glaze
- Salt and pepper to taste

Directions

1. Arrange tomato, mozzarella, and basil on a plate.
2. Drizzle with olive oil and balsamic glaze.
3. Season with salt and pepper.

Fun Facts

The combination of fresh mozzarella and basil makes this salad a delightful appetizer.

4 servings

250

20

Vegan Caesar Salad

Ingredients:

- 1 head Romaine lettuce, chopped
- 1 cup cherry tomatoes, halved
- 1/2 cup crispy chickpeas
- 1/4 cup nutritional yeast
- 1/4 cup tahini
- 2 tbsp lemon juice
- 2 cloves garlic, minced
- 2 tsp Dijon mustard
- 1/4 cup water
- Salt and pepper to taste

A plant-based take on the classic Caesar salad with a creamy tahini dressing and crispy chickpea croutons.

Directions

1. Toss lettuce, tomatoes, and chickpeas.
2. In a bowl, whisk nutritional yeast, tahini, lemon juice, garlic, mustard, and water.
3. Season with salt and pepper.
4. Drizzle dressing over the salad.

Fun Facts

Nutritional yeast and chickpeas add a cheesy and protein-packed twist to this vegan salad.

4 servings

320

30

Asian Sesame Noodle Salad

Ingredients:

- 8 oz cooked noodles (such as soba or udon)
- 1 cup bell peppers, thinly sliced
- 1 cup cucumber, julienned
- 1/2 cup carrots, julienned
- 1/4 cup scallions, sliced
- 2 tbsp toasted sesame seeds
- 1/4 cup soy sauce
- 2 tbsp rice vinegar
- 1 tbsp sesame oil
- 1 tbsp honey
- 1 clove garlic, minced
- Salt and pepper to taste

A refreshing noodle salad with a sesame soy dressing, topped with colorful veggies and toasted sesame seeds.

Directions

1. Combine cooked noodles, peppers, cucumber, carrots, and scallions.
2. In a bowl, whisk together soy sauce, rice vinegar, sesame oil, honey, garlic, salt, and pepper.
3. Toss the salad with the dressing.
4. Sprinkle with sesame seeds.

Fun Facts

Sesame seeds add a delightful crunch and nutty flavor to this Asian-inspired salad.

4
servings

220

15

Greek Salad

Ingredients:

- 2 cucumbers, sliced
- 4 tomatoes, chopped
- 1/2 red onion, thinly sliced
- 1/2 cup Kalamata olives, pitted
- 1/2 cup feta cheese, crumbled
- 1/4 cup fresh oregano leaves
- 2 tbsp extra-virgin olive oil
- 2 tbsp lemon juice
- Salt and pepper to taste

A classic Greek salad with crisp cucumbers, juicy tomatoes, olives, and feta cheese, drizzled with a lemon-oregano dressing.

Directions

1. Combine cucumbers, tomatoes, red onion, olives, and feta cheese.
2. In a bowl, whisk together olive oil, lemon juice, oregano, salt, and pepper.
3. Drizzle the dressing over the salad.

Fun Facts

Oregano and feta cheese provide an authentic Greek flavor to this salad.

4
servings

260

45

Roasted Beet Salad

Ingredients:

- 4 medium beets, roasted and diced
- 4 cups arugula
- 1/2 cup goat cheese, crumbled
- 1/2 cup candied pecans
- 1/4 cup balsamic vinegar
- 2 tbsp honey
- 2 tbsp extra-virgin olive oil
- Salt and pepper to taste

A colorful salad featuring roasted beets, arugula, goat cheese, and candied pecans, drizzled with a honey-balsamic vinaigrette.

Directions

1. Arrange beets, arugula, goat cheese, and pecans on a plate.
2. In a bowl, whisk together balsamic vinegar, honey, olive oil, salt, and pepper.
3. Drizzle the dressing over the salad.

Fun Facts

Beets are rich in antioxidants and vitamins, making this salad a nutritious choice.

4
servings

180

15

Spinach and Strawberry Salad

Ingredients:

- 4 cups fresh spinach
- 2 cups strawberries, sliced
- 1/4 cup red onion, thinly sliced
- 1/4 cup sliced almonds, toasted
- 1/4 cup balsamic vinegar
- 2 tbsp honey
- 2 tbsp extra-virgin olive oil
- Salt and pepper to taste

A sweet and tangy salad with fresh spinach, ripe strawberries, red onion, and a balsamic vinaigrette, topped with toasted almonds.

Directions

1. Toss together spinach, strawberries, red onion, and almonds.
2. In a bowl, whisk together balsamic vinegar, honey, olive oil, salt, and pepper.
3. Drizzle the dressing over the salad.

Fun Facts

Strawberries add a burst of sweetness and vitamin C to this spinach salad.

4
servings

320

30

Vegan Cobb Salad

A vegan version of the classic Cobb salad with avocado, tempeh bacon, and a dairy-free ranch dressing.

Ingredients:

- 4 cups mixed greens
- 2 avocados, diced
- 1 cup cherry tomatoes, halved
- 1/2 cup tempeh bacon, crumbled
- 1/2 cup corn kernels
- 1/4 cup red onion, finely chopped
- 1/4 cup dairy-free ranch dressing
- Salt and pepper to taste

Directions

1. Toss mixed greens with avocados, tomatoes, tempeh bacon, corn, and red onion.
2. Drizzle with dairy-free ranch dressing.
3. Season with salt and pepper.

Fun Facts

Tempeh bacon provides a smoky and savory element to this vegan Cobb salad.

4
servings

120

10

Cucumber and Tomato Salad

Ingredients:

- 4 cucumbers, sliced
- 4 tomatoes, chopped
- 1/4 cup red onion, finely chopped
- 2 tbsp fresh dill, chopped
- 2 tbsp white wine vinegar
- 2 tbsp extra-virgin olive oil
- Salt and pepper to taste

A light and refreshing salad with crisp cucumbers, juicy tomatoes, and a dill vinaigrette. Perfect as a side dish or quick snack.

Directions

1. Combine cucumbers, tomatoes, red onion, and dill.
2. In a bowl, whisk together white wine vinegar, olive oil, salt, and pepper.
3. Drizzle the dressing over the salad.

Fun Facts

Dill adds a refreshing and herby flavor to this simple cucumber and tomato salad.

Chapter 4:
Plant-Powered Bowls

2
servings

380

30

Buddha Bowl with Tahini Dressing

Ingredients:

- 1 cup cooked brown rice
- 1 cup roasted sweet potatoes
- 1 cup steamed broccoli
- 1 cup chickpeas, roasted
- 1 cup shredded carrots
- 1/4 cup tahini
- 2 tbsp lemon juice
- 2 tbsp water
- 1 clove garlic, minced
- 2 tsp soy sauce
- Salt and pepper to taste

A nourishing Buddha bowl filled with a colorful variety of vegetables, grains, and a creamy tahini dressing.

Directions

1. Divide rice between bowls.
2. Arrange sweet potatoes, broccoli, chickpeas, and carrots on top.
3. In a bowl, whisk together tahini, lemon juice, water, garlic, soy sauce, salt, and pepper.
4. Drizzle dressing over the bowls.

Fun Facts

Buddha bowls offer a balanced meal with a variety of nutrients in one dish.

2
servings

420

35

Vegan Burrito Bowl

A vegan take on the classic burrito, featuring rice, black beans, fajita veggies, salsa, and guacamole in a bowl format.

Ingredients:

- 1 cup cooked brown rice
- 1 cup black beans, cooked
- 1 cup fajita veggies (bell peppers, onions)
- 1/2 cup salsa
- 1/2 cup guacamole
- 1/4 cup vegan sour cream
- 1/4 cup fresh cilantro, chopped
- Salt and pepper to taste

Directions

1. Divide rice between bowls.
2. Top with black beans, fajita veggies, and salsa.
3. Add guacamole and vegan sour cream.
4. Garnish with cilantro.
5. Season with salt and pepper.

Fun Facts

Burrito bowls provide the flavors of a burrito without the tortilla, perfect for a gluten-free option.

2
servings

350

25

Vegan Poke Bowl

Ingredients:

- 1 cup cooked sushi rice
- 8 oz firm tofu, cubed
- 1/2 cup edamame, shelled
- 1/2 cup diced cucumber
- 1/2 cup diced mango
- 1/4 cup sliced radishes
- 2 tbsp soy sauce
- 1 tbsp rice vinegar
- 1 tsp fresh ginger, grated
- 1 tsp sesame oil
- 1 tsp maple syrup
- 1/4 cup sliced green onions
- 1 tsp sesame seeds
- Salt and pepper to taste

A vegan twist on a Hawaiian favorite, this poke bowl features marinated tofu, fresh vegetables, and sushi rice, drizzled with soy-ginger sauce.

Directions

1. Divide rice between bowls.
2. Marinate tofu in soy sauce, rice vinegar, ginger, sesame oil, maple syrup, salt, and pepper.
3. Top rice with tofu, edamame, cucumber, mango, and radishes.
4. Drizzle with the remaining marinade.
5. Garnish with green onions and sesame seeds.

Fun Facts

Poke bowls are a healthy and colorful option, full of fresh and vibrant ingredients.

2
servings

320

25

Quinoa and Chickpea Bowl

Ingredients:

- 1 cup cooked quinoa
- 1 cup roasted bell peppers and zucchini
- 1 cup chickpeas, roasted
- 1/4 cup tahini
- 2 tbsp lemon juice
- 2 tbsp water
- 1 clove garlic, minced
- Salt and pepper to taste

A protein-packed bowl featuring quinoa, chickpeas, roasted vegetables, and a lemon-tahini dressing.

Directions

1. Divide quinoa between bowls.
2. Arrange bell peppers, zucchini, and chickpeas on top.
3. In a bowl, whisk together tahini, lemon juice, water, garlic, salt, and pepper.
4. Drizzle dressing over the bowls.

Fun Facts

Quinoa and chickpeas provide a protein boost, making this bowl satisfying and nutritious.

2
servings

380

30

Sweet Potato and Black Bean Bowl

Ingredients:

- 2 cups roasted sweet potatoes
- 1 cup black beans, cooked
- 1 cup corn kernels
- 1 avocado, diced
- 1/4 cup fresh cilantro, chopped
- 1/4 cup chipotle-lime dressing
- Salt and pepper to taste

A hearty and spicy bowl with roasted sweet potatoes, black beans, corn, and avocado, topped with a chipotle-lime dressing.

Directions

1. Divide sweet potatoes between bowls.
2. Top with black beans, corn, and avocado.
3. Drizzle with chipotle-lime dressing.
4. Garnish with cilantro.
5. Season with salt and pepper.

Fun Facts

Sweet potatoes are a rich source of fiber and vitamins, making this bowl a healthy choice.

2
servings

350

30

Vegan Sushi Bowl

Ingredients:

- 1 cup cooked sushi rice
- 1 avocado, sliced
- 1/2 cucumber, julienned
- 2 sheets nori seaweed, torn into strips
- 1/4 cup soy sauce
- 1 tsp wasabi paste
- 1 tsp sesame oil
- 1 tsp maple syrup

Enjoy the flavors of sushi in a deconstructed bowl with sushi rice, avocado, cucumber, nori strips, and a soy-wasabi dressing.

Directions

1. Divide rice between bowls.
2. Top with avocado, cucumber, and nori strips.
3. In a bowl, whisk together soy sauce, wasabi paste, sesame oil, and maple syrup.
4. Drizzle dressing over the bowls.

Fun Facts

Sushi bowls offer the flavors of sushi without the need for rolling skills.

2
servings

320

30

Roasted Veggie and Hummus Bowl

Ingredients:

- 1 cup cooked quinoa
- 2 cups roasted mixed vegetables (e.g., bell peppers, eggplant, zucchini)
- 1/2 cup hummus
- 1/4 cup tahini
- 2 tbsp lemon juice
- 2 tbsp water
- 1 clove garlic, minced
- Salt and pepper to taste

A bowl of roasted vegetables, quinoa, hummus, and a lemon-tahini sauce, creating a satisfying and nutritious meal.

Directions

1. Divide quinoa between bowls.
2. Top with roasted vegetables and hummus.
3. In a bowl, whisk together tahini, lemon juice, water, garlic, salt, and pepper.
4. Drizzle dressing over the bowls.

Fun Facts

Hummus adds a creamy and protein-rich element to this roasted veggie bowl.

2
servings

400

35

Vegan Thai Green Curry Bowl

Ingredients:

- 1 cup cooked jasmine rice
- 8 oz firm tofu, cubed
- 1 cup bell peppers, sliced
- 1 cup snap peas, trimmed
- 1/2 cup Thai green curry sauce
- 1/4 cup fresh basil leaves
- Salt and pepper to taste

A vibrant and flavorful Thai green curry bowl with tofu, vegetables, and jasmine rice, perfect for a spicy and aromatic meal.

Directions

1. Divide rice between bowls.
2. In a pan, sauté tofu, bell peppers, and snap peas until slightly browned.
3. Stir in Thai green curry sauce and cook until heated through.
4. Top rice with the curry mixture.
5. Garnish with fresh basil.
6. Season with salt and pepper.

Fun Facts

Thai green curry sauce provides a fragrant and spicy kick to this bowl.

2
servings

340

30

Mediterranean Rice Bowl

A Mediterranean-inspired rice bowl with falafel, tzatziki, fresh vegetables, and a lemon-olive dressing.

Ingredients:

- 1 cup cooked basmati rice
- 4 falafel, heated
- 1/2 cup cherry tomatoes, halved
- 1/2 cucumber, diced
- 1/4 cup red onion, finely chopped
- 1/4 cup tzatziki
- 2 tbsp Kalamata olives, pitted and sliced
- 1/4 cup lemon-olive dressing
- Salt and pepper to taste

Directions

1. Divide rice between bowls.
2. Top with falafel, cherry tomatoes, cucumber, red onion, and tzatziki.
3. Drizzle with lemon-olive dressing.
4. Garnish with Kalamata olives.
5. Season with salt and pepper.

Fun Facts

Falafel adds a crispy and flavorful element to this Mediterranean rice bowl.

2
servings

380

35

Vegan BBQ Bowl

A smoky and savory BBQ bowl with barbecue tempeh, corn, coleslaw, and roasted sweet potatoes, drizzled with vegan ranch dressing.

Ingredients:

- 1 cup roasted sweet potatoes
- 8 oz barbecue tempeh, sliced
- 1 cup corn kernels
- 1 cup coleslaw
- 1/4 cup vegan ranch dressing
- Salt and pepper to taste

Directions

1. Divide sweet potatoes between bowls.
2. Top with barbecue tempeh, corn, and coleslaw.
3. Drizzle with vegan ranch dressing.
4. Season with salt and pepper.

Fun Facts

Barbecue tempeh adds a smoky and hearty flavor to this vegan BBQ bowl.

We have a small favor to ask

My dear fellow plant-based enthusiasts,

As we saunter through the garden of "Plant-Based 5-Ingredient," I hope you've unearthed a wealth of effortless, healthful recipes that have stirred your taste buds and invigorated your passion for wholesome living. This book is a celebration of the simplicity and vitality that a plant-based lifestyle can offer.

We've embarked on a flavorful journey with over 100 recipes, each meticulously designed to bring you the best of plant-based cooking without the fuss. We've indulged in the vibrant colors and nourishing ingredients that nature provides, creating dishes that are as kind to your taste buds as they are to your well-being.

But now, my friends, we find ourselves at a crossroads, and we humbly request your assistance. You see, reviews are the lifeblood of small publishers like us. Your star ratings, your succinct sentiments, your candid feedback, and your constructive criticism have the power to uplift us and propel us forward in the world of plant-based cuisine.

So, if I may ask, when you have a moment, please take a slight detour back to the app or platform where you first discovered this book. There, you'll find a precious button—the one that says "Review." We ask that you bestow upon us a rating, along with a few words from your heart. We read each and every review, and your insights are held in the highest regard. Your feedback is the compass that guides us to new culinary horizons.

In the universe of cooking, we know that, like a rogue tomato in a salad, the occasional imperfection may sneak in. We've done our utmost to provide you with recipes that shine, but sometimes, a spice may be a tad bold, or a baking time may err. We're hopeful that your culinary skills have helped finesse these minor hiccups, and we appreciate your understanding.

Looking ahead, we pledge to keep crafting cookbooks that make the plant-based lifestyle more accessible, vibrant, and delightful. Your reviews, my friends, are the seeds of our future growth.

In conclusion, I extend my deepest gratitude to you for sharing this journey with us. Your culinary creations have been a testament to the boundless creativity of plant-based cooking.

May your kitchens forever bloom with the colors of plant-based vitality, your lives resonate with the melody of good health, and your reviews inspire others to join the journey to a better world.

Now, let's get back to those delightful recipes, shall we?

Yours in flavor and vitality,

Garden of Grapes

Chapter 5:
Easy Pasta Delights

2
servings

400

20

Vegan Pesto Pasta

Ingredients:

- 8 oz pasta (such as spaghetti or fettuccine)
- 2 cups fresh basil leaves
- 1/2 cup pine nuts
- 2 cloves garlic
- 1/2 cup extra-virgin olive oil
- 1/2 cup nutritional yeast
- 2 tbsp lemon juice
- Salt and pepper to taste

A classic pesto pasta made vegan with a rich basil and pine nut sauce, perfect for a quick and flavorful meal.

Directions

1. Cook pasta according to package instructions.
2. In a food processor, blend basil, pine nuts, garlic, olive oil, nutritional yeast, lemon juice, salt, and pepper until smooth.
3. Toss pasta with pesto sauce.

Fun Facts

Nutritional yeast adds a cheesy flavor to this vegan pesto, making it dairy-free and delicious.

2
servings

420

25

Vegan Alfredo Pasta

Ingredients:

- 8 oz pasta (such as fettuccine or linguine)
- 1 cup raw cashews, soaked
- 1 cup water- 2 cloves garlic
- 1/4 cup nutritional yeast
- 2 tbsp lemon juice
- 1/2 tsp salt
- 1/4 tsp nutmeg
- 1/4 tsp black pepper

A creamy and indulgent Alfredo pasta made vegan with a cashew cream sauce, perfect for a comforting and satisfying dish.

Directions

1. Cook pasta according to package instructions.
2. In a blender, combine soaked cashews, water, garlic, nutritional yeast, lemon juice, salt, nutmeg, and black pepper. Blend until smooth.
3. Toss pasta with the cashew Alfredo sauce.

Fun Facts

Cashew cream creates a luscious and dairy-free Alfredo sauce, perfect for a vegan pasta dish.

2
servings

350

15

Vegan Spaghetti Aglio e Olio

A simple yet flavorful pasta dish with spaghetti, garlic, red pepper flakes, and olive oil, providing a spicy and garlicky kick.

Ingredients:

- 8 oz spaghetti
- 4 cloves garlic, thinly sliced
- 1/4 tsp red pepper flakes
- 1/4 cup extra-virgin olive oil
- Salt and pepper to taste

Directions

1. Cook spaghetti according to package instructions.
2. In a pan, sauté garlic and red pepper flakes in olive oil until garlic is golden.
3. Toss cooked spaghetti with the garlic and oil mixture.
4. Season with salt and pepper.

Fun Facts

Spaghetti Aglio e Olio is a classic Italian dish that's simple yet incredibly flavorful.

4
servings

320

30

One-Pot Vegan Chili Mac

Ingredients:

- 8 oz elbow macaroni
- 1 can (15 oz) vegan chili
- 1 cup vegan cheddar cheese, shredded
- 1/4 cup diced green onions
- Salt and pepper to taste

A hearty and comforting one-pot chili mac with pasta, plant-based chili, and vegan cheese, perfect for a spicy and satisfying meal.

Directions

1. In a large pot, cook macaroni according to package instructions.
2. Add vegan chili and cheese to the cooked macaroni.
3. Cook over low heat, stirring until cheese is melted.
4. Top with green onions.
5. Season with salt and pepper.

Fun Facts

One-pot chili mac is a quick and easy comfort food that combines the flavors of chili and macaroni and cheese.

2
servings

380

20

Vegan Lemon Asparagus Pasta

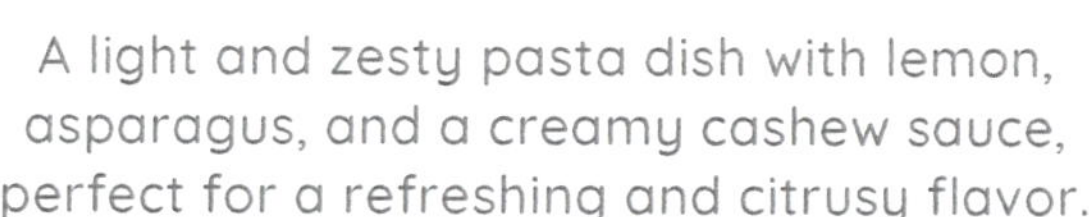

Ingredients:

- 8 oz pasta (such as linguine or tagliatelle)
- 1 bunch asparagus, trimmed and cut into pieces
- 1 cup raw cashews, soaked
- 1/2 cup water
- 2 cloves garlic
- 1/4 cup lemon juice
- 2 tbsp nutritional yeast
- 1/2 tsp salt
- 1/4 tsp black pepper

A light and zesty pasta dish with lemon, asparagus, and a creamy cashew sauce, perfect for a refreshing and citrusy flavor.

Directions

1. Cook pasta according to package instructions.
2. In a pan, sauté asparagus until tender.
3. In a blender, combine soaked cashews, water, garlic, lemon juice, nutritional yeast, salt, and black pepper. Blend until creamy.
4. Toss cooked pasta with asparagus and lemon-cashew sauce.

Fun Facts

Cashew cream adds a rich and creamy texture to this vegan lemon asparagus pasta.

4 servings

380

25

Vegan Mac and Cheese

Ingredients:

- 8 oz elbow macaroni
- 2 cups unsweetened almond milk
- 1 cup raw cashews, soaked
- 1/4 cup nutritional yeast
- 2 cloves garlic
- 1/2 tsp salt
- 1/4 tsp turmeric
- 1/4 tsp paprika
- 1/4 tsp black pepper

A classic mac and cheese made vegan with a creamy sauce, nutritional yeast, and elbow macaroni, perfect for a comforting and cheesy dish.

Directions

1. Cook macaroni according to package instructions.
2. In a blender, combine almond milk, soaked cashews, nutritional yeast, garlic, salt, turmeric, paprika, and black pepper. Blend until smooth.
3. Toss cooked macaroni with the vegan cheese sauce.

Fun Facts

Nutritional yeast and cashews create a creamy and cheesy flavor in this vegan mac and cheese.

2
servings

360

20

Vegan Peanut Noodles

Ingredients:

- 8 oz rice noodles
- 8 oz firm tofu, cubed
- 1/2 cup bell peppers, thinly sliced
- 1/2 cup carrots, julienned
- 1/4 cup fresh cilantro, chopped
- 1/4 cup peanuts, chopped
- 1/4 cup green onions, sliced
- 1/4 cup peanut sauce
- Salt and pepper to taste

A quick and savory noodle dish with a peanut sauce, fresh vegetables, and tofu, perfect for a flavorful and satisfying meal.

Directions

1. Cook rice noodles according to package instructions.
2. In a pan, sauté tofu until lightly browned.
3. Toss cooked noodles with tofu, bell peppers, carrots, cilantro, peanuts, and green onions.
4. Drizzle with peanut sauce.
5. Season with salt and pepper.

Fun Facts

Peanut sauce adds a delicious and nutty flavor to this vegan noodle dish.

2
servings

340

20

Vegan Garlic and Mushroom Pasta

Ingredients:

- 8 oz pasta (such as penne or linguine)
- 8 oz mushrooms, sliced
- 1/2 cup unsweetened almond milk
- 2 cloves garlic, minced
- 2 tbsp nutritional yeast
- 1/2 tsp salt
- 1/4 tsp black pepper

A comforting pasta dish with garlic, sautéed mushrooms, and a creamy almond sauce, perfect for a savory and satisfying flavor.

Directions

1. Cook pasta according to package instructions.
2. In a pan, sauté mushrooms until they release their moisture.
3. Add garlic and cook until fragrant.
4. Stir in almond milk, nutritional yeast, salt, and black pepper.
5. Toss cooked pasta with the mushroom and garlic sauce.

Fun Facts

Almond milk creates a creamy and dairy-free sauce in this vegan garlic and mushroom pasta.

2
servings

360

20

Vegan Spinach and Artichoke Pasta

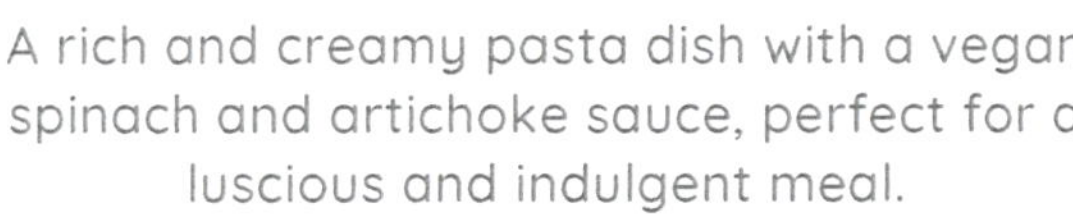

Ingredients:

- 8 oz pasta (such as fettuccine or rigatoni)
- 1 cup raw cashews, soaked
- 1 cup unsweetened almond milk
- 1/4 cup nutritional yeast
- 1/2 cup frozen spinach, thawed and squeezed
- 1/2 cup artichoke hearts, chopped
- 2 cloves garlic
- 1/2 tsp salt
- 1/4 tsp black pepper

A rich and creamy pasta dish with a vegan spinach and artichoke sauce, perfect for a luscious and indulgent meal.

Directions

1. Cook pasta according to package instructions.
2. In a blender, combine soaked cashews, almond milk, nutritional yeast, spinach, artichoke hearts, garlic, salt, and black pepper. Blend until creamy.
3. Toss cooked pasta with the vegan spinach and artichoke sauce.

Fun Facts

Spinach and artichoke hearts create a rich and creamy texture in this vegan pasta dish.

2
servings

320

15

Vegan Tomato Basil Pasta

Ingredients:

- 8 oz pasta (such as penne or spaghetti)
- 1 can (15 oz) crushed tomatoes
- 1/4 cup fresh basil, chopped
- 2 cloves garlic, minced
- 1/4 cup extra-virgin olive oil
- 1/4 tsp red pepper flakes
- Salt and pepper to taste

A quick and flavorful pasta with a tomato and basil sauce, perfect for a classic and delicious meal.

Directions

1. Cook pasta according to package instructions.
2. In a pan, sauté garlic and red pepper flakes in olive oil until garlic is fragrant.
3. Stir in crushed tomatoes and basil.
4. Toss cooked pasta with the tomato and basil sauce.
5. Season with salt and pepper.

Fun Facts

Tomato and basil make a classic and timeless combination in this vegan pasta dish.

Chapter 6:
Veggie-Filled Wraps and Sandwiches

2
servings

320

15

Vegan Chickpea Salad Sandwich

Ingredients:

- 1 can (15 oz) chickpeas, drained and mashed
- 1/4 cup vegan mayonnaise
- 2 stalks celery, finely chopped
- 1/4 cup red onion, finely chopped
- 2 tbsp fresh dill, chopped
- 2 tbsp fresh parsley, chopped
- 2 tsp Dijon mustard
- Salt and pepper to taste
- 4 slices whole-grain bread
- Lettuce and tomato slices (optional)

A delightful and protein-packed chickpea salad sandwich with creamy vegan mayo, celery, and fresh herbs, perfect for a satisfying and plant-based meal.

Directions

1. In a bowl, combine mashed chickpeas, vegan mayonnaise, celery, red onion, dill, parsley, Dijon mustard, salt, and pepper.
2. Spread the chickpea salad on slices of whole-grain bread.
3. Add lettuce and tomato slices if desired.
4. Assemble into sandwiches.

Fun Facts

Chickpeas provide a satisfying and protein-rich base for this vegan salad sandwich.

2
servings

380

20

Vegan BLT Wrap

Ingredients:

- 6 oz smoky tempeh bacon
- 2 large tortillas
- 2 tbsp vegan mayonnaise
- 4 lettuce leaves
- 8 tomato slices

A classic BLT wrap made vegan with smoky tempeh bacon, lettuce, tomato, and vegan mayo, perfect for a savory and crispy delight.

Directions

1. In a pan, cook smoky tempeh bacon until crispy.
2. Spread vegan mayonnaise on the tortillas.
3. Place lettuce leaves, tomato slices, and cooked tempeh bacon on each tortilla.
4. Roll into wraps.

Fun Facts

Smoky tempeh bacon adds a delicious and savory flavor to this vegan BLT wrap.

2
servings

350

25

Vegan BBQ Jackfruit Sandwich

Ingredients:

- 2 cups canned young jackfruit, drained and shredded
- 1/2 cup vegan BBQ sauce
- 2 large buns
- 1 cup coleslaw
- 1/4 cup pickles, sliced

A smoky and satisfying BBQ jackfruit sandwich with tender jackfruit, coleslaw, and pickles, perfect for a tangy and plant-based treat.

Directions

1. In a pan, sauté shredded jackfruit until heated.
2. Stir in vegan BBQ sauce and cook until jackfruit is coated.
3. Toast the buns.
4. Assemble the sandwiches with BBQ jackfruit, coleslaw, and pickles.

Fun Facts

Jackfruit has a meaty texture and is perfect for vegan BBQ sandwiches, providing a smoky and tender taste.

2
servings

320

20

Vegan Egg Salad Wrap

A vegan take on the classic egg salad wrap with tofu, vegan mayo, mustard, and fresh chives, perfect for a creamy and nostalgic flavor.

Ingredients:

- 8 oz extra-firm tofu, crumbled
- 1/4 cup vegan mayonnaise
- 2 tsp Dijon mustard
- 2 tsp fresh chives, chopped
- 1/2 tsp black salt (kala namak, for an eggy flavor)
- Salt and pepper to taste
- 2 large tortillas
- Lettuce and tomato slices (optional)

Directions

1. In a bowl, combine crumbled tofu, vegan mayonnaise, Dijon mustard, chives, black salt, salt, and pepper.
2. Spread the tofu egg salad on the tortillas.
3. Add lettuce and tomato slices if desired.
4. Roll into wraps.

Fun Facts

Black salt provides an eggy flavor to this vegan egg salad, making it taste just like the classic version.

2
servings

340

25

Vegan Portobello Mushroom Burger

Ingredients:

- 2 large Portobello mushrooms, stems removed
- 2 whole-grain burger buns
- 1/4 cup tahini
- 2 tbsp lemon juice
- 1 tsp smoked paprika
- Salt and pepper to taste
- Lettuce, tomato slices, and red onion slices (optional)

A hearty and umami-filled Portobello mushroom burger with a smoky tahini sauce, perfect for a satisfying and meaty plant-based meal.

Directions

1. In a bowl, whisk together tahini, lemon juice, smoked paprika, salt, and pepper.
2. Brush the Portobello mushrooms with the tahini sauce.
3. Grill or broil mushrooms until tender.
4. Toast the burger buns.
5. Assemble the burgers with lettuce, tomato slices, and red onion slices if desired.

Fun Facts

Portobello mushrooms offer a meaty and flavorful patty for this vegan burger, enhanced by smoky tahini sauce.

2
servings

350

25

Vegan Buffalo Cauliflower Wrap

Ingredients:

- 4 cups cauliflower florets
- 1/2 cup Buffalo sauce
- 2 large tortillas
- 1/4 cup vegan ranch dressing
- 1 cup lettuce, chopped
- 1/2 cup carrots, julienned

A spicy and crispy Buffalo cauliflower wrap with creamy vegan ranch dressing, perfect for a fiery and flavorful plant-based treat.

Directions

1. In a bowl, toss cauliflower florets with Buffalo sauce.
2. Roast in the oven until crispy.
3. Spread vegan ranch dressing on the tortillas.
4. Place roasted cauliflower, lettuce, and carrots on each tortilla.
5. Roll into wraps.

Fun Facts

Buffalo cauliflower provides a spicy and crunchy texture in this vegan wrap, balanced by creamy ranch dressing.

2
servings

360

20

Vegan Mediterranean Wrap

Ingredients:

- 2 large tortillas
- 1/2 cup hummus
- 1 cup cucumbers, diced
- 1 cup tomatoes, diced
- 1/4 cup Kalamata olives, pitted and sliced
- 2 tbsp fresh mint, chopped
- 2 tbsp fresh parsley, chopped
- Salt and pepper to taste

A fresh and colorful Mediterranean wrap with hummus, cucumbers, tomatoes, olives, and fresh herbs, perfect for a light and flavorful meal.

Directions

1. Spread hummus on the tortillas.
2. Add cucumbers, tomatoes, Kalamata olives, mint, parsley, salt, and pepper to each tortilla.
3. Roll into wraps.

Fun Facts

Mediterranean wraps offer a light and refreshing taste with a variety of fresh vegetables and herbs.

2
servings

380

20

Vegan Avocado and Hummus Wrap

A creamy and nutritious wrap with avocado, hummus, spinach, and bell peppers, perfect for a wholesome and satisfying plant-based meal.

Ingredients:

- 2 large tortillas
- 1 avocado, sliced
- 1/2 cup hummus
- 2 cups fresh spinach leaves
- 1/2 cup bell peppers, sliced
- Salt and pepper to taste

Directions

1. Lay out tortillas and add avocado slices.
2. Spread hummus on top of the avocado.
3. Add fresh spinach leaves and bell pepper slices.
4. Season with salt and pepper.
5. Roll into wraps.

Fun Facts

Avocado and hummus create a creamy and nutritious combination in this vegan wrap, full of healthy fats and protein.

2
servings

360

20

Vegan Caprese Panini

Ingredients:

- 4 slices whole-grain bread
- 1/2 cup vegan mozzarella slices
- 1 cup tomato slices
- 1/2 cup fresh basil leaves
- 2 tbsp balsamic glaze

A delightful and melty Caprese panini with vegan mozzarella, tomatoes, fresh basil, and balsamic glaze, perfect for a cheesy and Italian-inspired delight.

Directions

1. On each slice of bread, layer vegan mozzarella, tomato slices, and fresh basil leaves.
2. Drizzle with balsamic glaze.
3. Close the sandwiches.
4. Grill in a panini press or on a stovetop grill until bread is crispy and cheese is melted.

Fun Facts

Caprese panini offers a cheesy and melty delight with the classic combination of tomatoes, mozzarella, and basil.

2
servings

340

30

Vegan Falafel Pita

Ingredients:

- 2 whole-grain pita breads
- 8 falafel patties
- 1/2 cup vegan tzatziki
- 1/2 cup cucumber, diced
- 1/2 cup tomatoes, diced
- 1/4 cup red onion, finely chopped
- 1/4 cup fresh parsley, chopped
- Salt and pepper to taste

A flavorful and satisfying falafel pita with homemade vegan tzatziki, fresh vegetables, and chickpea patties, perfect for a Middle Eastern-inspired treat.

Directions

1. Warm pita breads in the oven.
2. Cut each pita in half and gently open the pocket.
3. Stuff each pita with falafel patties, vegan tzatziki, cucumber, tomatoes, red onion, parsley, salt, and pepper.

Fun Facts

Falatel and vegan tzatziki provide a tasty and traditional Middle Eastern flavor in this pita sandwich.

Chapter 7:
Flavorful Stir-Fries

2
servings

340

20

Tofu and Broccoli Stir-Fry

A classic tofu and broccoli stir-fry with a savory sauce, perfect for a quick and satisfying plant-based meal.

Ingredients:

- 8 oz firm tofu, cubed
- 2 cups broccoli florets
- 1/2 cup bell peppers, sliced
- 1/4 cup scallions, chopped
- 1/4 cup soy sauce
- 2 tbsp hoisin sauce
- 1 tbsp rice vinegar
- 2 tsp brown sugar
- 2 cloves garlic, minced
1 tsp ginger, minced
- 1 tbsp cornstarch
- 2 tbsp vegetable oil

Directions

1. In a bowl, whisk together soy sauce, hoisin sauce, rice vinegar, brown sugar, and cornstarch.
2. In a wok or large pan, heat vegetable oil over medium-high heat.
3. Add tofu and cook until golden.
4. Remove tofu from the pan.
5. In the same pan, add garlic and ginger, and stir-fry for a minute.
6. Add broccoli, bell peppers, and scallions, and stir-fry until crisp-tender.
7. Return tofu to the pan.
8. Pour the sauce over the stir-fry and cook until thickened.

Fun Facts

Tofu and broccoli create a delicious and protein-packed combination in this classic stir-fry.

2
servings

360

25

Vegan Teriyaki Tofu Stir-Fry

Ingredients:

- 8 oz firm tofu, cubed
- 2 cups mixed bell peppers, sliced
- 1 cup snap peas, trimmed
- 1/2 cup carrots, julienned
- 1/4 cup teriyaki sauce
- 1 tbsp soy sauce
- 1 tbsp rice vinegar
- 1 tbsp brown sugar
- 1 tbsp vegetable oil

Fun Facts

Teriyaki sauce adds a sweet and salty flavor to this vegan tofu stir-fry, making it a delicious and satisfying dish.

A sweet and savory teriyaki tofu stir-fry with colorful vegetables, perfect for a flavorful and satisfying plant-based dish.

Directions

1. In a bowl, combine teriyaki sauce, soy sauce, rice vinegar, brown sugar, and a bit of water.
2. In a wok or large pan, heat vegetable oil over medium-high heat.
3. Add tofu and cook until golden.
4. Remove tofu from the pan.
5. In the same pan, add mixed bell peppers, snap peas, and carrots, and stir-fry until crisp-tender.
6. Return tofu to the pan.
7. Pour the teriyaki sauce mixture over the stir-fry and cook until heated through.

2
servings

380

30

Vegan Pineapple Fried Rice

Ingredients:

- 8 oz firm tofu, cubed
- 1 cup cooked jasmine rice
- 1/2 cup pineapple chunks
- 1/2 cup mixed bell peppers, diced
- 1/4 cup green peas
- 1/4 cup red onion, finely chopped
- 1/4 cup cashews, chopped
- 2 cloves garlic, minced
- 1 tsp curry powder
- 2 tbsp soy sauce
- 1 tbsp vegetable oil

Fun Facts

Pineapple adds a sweet and tropical twist to this vegan fried rice, creating a colorful and flavorful dish.

A tropical and colorful pineapple fried rice with tofu, veggies, and a touch of curry, perfect for a delightful and exotic plant-based meal.

Directions

1. In a wok or large pan, heat vegetable oil over medium-high heat.
2. Add tofu and cook until golden.
3. Remove tofu from the pan.
4. In the same pan, add garlic and curry powder, and stir-fry for a minute.
5. Add cooked jasmine rice and stir-fry until heated.
6. Stir in pineapple chunks, mixed bell peppers, green peas, red onion, and cashews.
7. Return tofu to the pan.
8. Drizzle with soy sauce and stir-fry until well combined.

2
servings

360

25

Vegan Cashew Vegetable Stir-Fry

Ingredients:

- 1 cup broccoli florets
- 1 cup mixed bell peppers, sliced
- 1/2 cup snap peas, trimmed
- 1/2 cup carrots, julienned
- 1/4 cup cashews
- 1/4 cup scallions, chopped
- 1/4 cup soy sauce
- 2 tbsp hoisin sauce
- 2 tbsp rice vinegar
- 1 tbsp brown sugar
- 2 cloves garlic, minced
- 1 tsp ginger, minced
- 1 tbsp cornstarch
- 2 tbsp vegetable oil

Fun Facts

Cashews provide a delightful crunch and protein boost to this vegan vegetable stir-fry.

A nutty and crunchy cashew vegetable stir-fry with a savory sauce, perfect for a satisfying and protein-packed plant-based meal.

Directions

1. In a bowl, whisk together soy sauce, hoisin sauce, rice vinegar, brown sugar, and cornstarch.
2. In a wok or large pan, heat vegetable oil over medium-high heat.
3. Add broccoli, mixed bell peppers, snap peas, and carrots, and stir-fry until crisp-tender.
4. Stir in cashews and scallions.
5. Add garlic and ginger, and stir-fry for a minute.
6. Pour the sauce over the stir-fry and cook until thickened.

2
servings

380

25

Vegan Kung Pao Tofu Stir-Fry

Ingredients:

- 8 oz firm tofu, cubed
- 1/2 cup mixed bell peppers, diced
- 1/2 cup snap peas, trimmed
- 1/4 cup peanuts
- 1/4 cup scallions, chopped
- 1/4 cup soy sauce
- 2 tbsp hoisin sauce
- 1 tbsp rice vinegar
- 1 tbsp brown sugar
- 1 tsp Szechuan peppercorns
- 2 cloves garlic, minced
- 1 tsp ginger, minced
- 1 tbsp cornstarch
- 2 tbsp vegetable oil

Fun Facts

Kung Pao tofu stir-fry offers a spicy and nutty flavor with a satisfying crunch from the peanuts.

A spicy and nutty Kung Pao tofu stir-fry with peanuts and colorful veggies, perfect for a fiery and satisfying plant-based dish.

Directions

1. In a bowl, whisk together soy sauce, hoisin sauce, rice vinegar, brown sugar, and cornstarch.
2. In a wok or large pan, heat vegetable oil over medium-high heat.
3. Add tofu and cook until golden.
4. Remove tofu from the pan.
5. In the same pan, add garlic, ginger, and Szechuan peppercorns, and stir-fry for a minute.
6. Add mixed bell peppers, snap peas, and scallions, and stir-fry until crisp-tender.
7. Return tofu to the pan.
8. Pour the sauce over the stir-fry and cook until thickened.
9. Top with peanuts.

2
servings

360

25

Vegan Thai Basil Stir-Fry

Ingredients:

- 8 oz firm tofu, cubed
- 1/2 cup mixed bell peppers, sliced
- 1/2 cup snap peas, trimmed
- 1/4 cup Thai holy basil leaves
- 2 cloves garlic, minced
- 2 red Thai chilies, sliced (adjust to taste)
- 1/4 cup soy sauce
- 1 tbsp hoisin sauce
- 1 tbsp rice vinegar
- 1 tbsp brown sugar
- 2 tbsp vegetable oil

Fun Facts

Thai holy basil adds a bold and aromatic flavor to this vegan stir-fry, creating a zesty and fragrant dish.

A zesty and aromatic Thai basil stir-fry with tofu and Thai holy basil, perfect for a bold and fragrant plant-based meal.

Directions

1. In a wok or large pan, heat vegetable oil over medium-high heat.
2. Add tofu and cook until golden.
3. Remove tofu from the pan.
4. In the same pan, add garlic and red Thai chilies, and stir-fry for a minute.
5. Add mixed bell peppers and snap peas, and stir-fry until crisp-tender.
6. Return tofu to the pan.
7. Stir in Thai holy basil leaves.
8. In a bowl, whisk together soy sauce, hoisin sauce, rice vinegar, and brown sugar.
9. Pour the sauce over the stir-fry and cook until heated through.

2
servings

380

25

Vegan Mongolian Seitan Stir-Fry

Ingredients:

- 8 oz seitan, sliced
- 1 cup green beans, trimmed
- 1/2 cup mixed bell peppers, sliced
- 1/4 cup scallions, chopped
- 2 cloves garlic, minced
- 1/4 cup soy sauce
- 2 tbsp hoisin sauce
- 1 tbsp rice vinegar
- 1 tbsp brown sugar
- 1 tbsp vegetable oil

A savory and umami-packed Mongolian seitan stir-fry with green beans and a rich sauce, perfect for a hearty and satisfying plant-based dish.

Directions

1. In a wok or large pan, heat vegetable oil over medium-high heat.
2. Add seitan and cook until slightly crispy.
3. Remove seitan from the pan.
4. In the same pan, add garlic and scallions, and stir-fry for a minute.
5. Add green beans and mixed bell peppers, and stir-fry until crisp-tender.
6. Return seitan to the pan.
7. In a bowl, whisk together soy sauce, hoisin sauce, rice vinegar, and brown sugar.
8. Pour the sauce over the stir-fry and cook until heated through.

Fun Facts

Seitan offers a meaty and umami-rich base in this Mongolian stir-fry, creating a hearty and satisfying dish.

2
servings

340

25

Vegan Szechuan Eggplant Stir-Fry

Ingredients:

- 8 oz firm tofu, cubed
- 2 cups Chinese eggplant, sliced
- 1/2 cup mixed bell peppers, sliced
- 1/4 cup scallions, chopped
- 2 cloves garlic, minced
- 2 red Thai chilies, sliced (adjust to taste)
- 1/4 cup soy sauce
- 2 tbsp hoisin sauce
- 1 tbsp rice vinegar
- 1 tbsp brown sugar
- 2 tbsp vegetable oil

Fun Facts

Szechuan eggplant provides a spicy and bold kick to this vegan stir-fry, making it a fiery and flavorful dish.

A spicy and flavorful Szechuan eggplant stir-fry with tofu and a bold sauce, perfect for a fiery and satisfying plant-based meal.

Directions

1. In a wok or large pan, heat vegetable oil over medium-high heat.
2. Add tofu and cook until golden.
3. Remove tofu from the pan.
4. In the same pan, add garlic and red Thai chilies, and stir-fry for a minute.
5. Add Chinese eggplant, mixed bell peppers, and scallions, and stir-fry until eggplant is tender.
6. Return tofu to the pan.
7. In a bowl, whisk together soy sauce, hoisin sauce, rice vinegar, and brown sugar.
8. Pour the sauce over the stir-fry and cook until heated through.

2
servings

360

25

Vegan Lemongrass Tofu Stir-Fry

Ingredients:

- 8 oz firm tofu, cubed
- 1/2 cup mixed bell peppers, sliced
- 1/2 cup snap peas, trimmed
- 1/4 cup scallions, chopped
- 2 cloves garlic, minced
- 2 tbsp lemongrass paste
- 1/4 cup soy sauce
- 2 tbsp brown sugar
- 1 tbsp vegetable oil

Fun Facts

Lemongrass paste adds a refreshing and citrusy note to this vegan tofu stir-fry, creating an aromatic and flavorful dish.

A fragrant and citrusy lemongrass tofu stir-fry with colorful veggies, perfect for a refreshing and aromatic plant-based meal.

Directions

1. In a wok or large pan, heat vegetable oil over medium-high heat.
2. Add tofu and cook until golden.
3. Remove tofu from the pan.
4. In the same pan, add garlic and lemongrass paste, and stir-fry for a minute.
5. Add mixed bell peppers, snap peas, and scallions, and stir-fry until crisp-tender.
6. Return tofu to the pan.
7. In a bowl, whisk together soy sauce and brown sugar.
8. Pour the sauce over the stir-fry and cook until heated through.

2
servings

340

30

Vegan Sweet and Sour Tempeh Stir-Fry

Ingredients:

- 8 oz tempeh, cubed
- 1/2 cup pineapple chunks
- 1/2 cup mixed bell peppers, sliced
- 1/4 cup red onion, finely chopped
- 2 cloves garlic, minced
- 1/4 cup ketchup
- 1/4 cup rice vinegar
- 2 tbsp brown sugar
- 1 tbsp soy sauce
- 1 tbsp vegetable oil

A tangy and colorful sweet and sour tempeh stir-fry with pineapple and bell peppers, perfect for a zesty and satisfying plant-based meal.

Directions

1. In a wok or large pan, heat vegetable oil over medium-high heat.
2. Add tempeh and cook until slightly crispy.
3. Remove tempeh from the pan.
4. In the same pan, add garlic and red onion, and stir-fry for a minute.
5. Add mixed bell peppers and pineapple chunks, and stir-fry until crisp-tender.
6. Return tempeh to the pan.
7. In a bowl, whisk together ketchup, rice vinegar, brown sugar, and soy sauce.
8. Pour the sauce over the stir-fry and cook until heated through.

Fun Facts

Sweet and sour sauce adds a tangy and vibrant flavor to this vegan tempeh stir-fry, creating a zesty and colorful dish.

Chapter 8:
Hearty and Wholesome Mains

4
servings

380

45

Vegan Lentil Shepherd's Pie

Ingredients:

- 1 cup green or brown lentils
- 4 cups vegetable broth
- 1 cup carrots, diced
- 1 cup peas
- 1/2 cup onions, chopped
- 2 cloves garlic, minced
- 1 tbsp tomato paste
- 2 tsp thyme
- 4 cups mashed potatoes (prepared separately)
- Salt and pepper to taste
- 2 tbsp olive oil

Fun Facts

Lentil Shepherd's Pie is a plant-based twist on a classic comfort dish, perfect for a satisfying and wholesome meal.

A comforting and vegan Lentil Shepherd's Pie with a savory lentil filling and creamy mashed potatoes, perfect for a hearty and wholesome meal.

Directions

1. In a large pot, combine lentils and vegetable broth. Bring to a boil, then reduce heat and simmer for 25-30 minutes until lentils are tender.
2. In a skillet, heat olive oil over medium heat. Add onions and garlic, and sauté until softened.
3. Stir in carrots, peas, tomato paste, and thyme. Cook for another 5 minutes.
4. Combine the cooked lentils with the vegetable mixture. Season with salt and pepper.
5. Preheat the oven to 400°F (200°C).
6. Transfer the lentil filling into a baking dish.
7. Spread the mashed potatoes on top.
8. Bake for 20-25 minutes until the top is golden.

4
servings

360

30

Vegan Chickpea Curry

Ingredients:

- 2 cans (15 oz each) chickpeas, drained
- 1 cup onions, chopped
- 2 cloves garlic, minced
- 1 tbsp ginger, minced
- 1 can (14 oz) diced tomatoes
- 1/4 cup tomato sauce
- 1 cup coconut milk
- 2 tbsp curry powder
- 1 tsp turmeric
- 1 tsp cumin
- 1 tsp paprika
- Salt and pepper to taste
- 2 tbsp vegetable oil

A flavorful and vegan Chickpea Curry with a rich tomato-based sauce, perfect for a spicy and protein-packed plant-based dish.

Directions

1. In a large skillet, heat vegetable oil over medium heat.
2. Add onions and sauté until soft.
3. Stir in garlic and ginger, and cook for another minute.
4. Add chickpeas, diced tomatoes, tomato sauce, coconut milk, and all the spices.
5. Simmer for 15-20 minutes until the sauce thickens.
6. Season with salt and pepper.
7. Serve over rice or with naan bread.

Fun Facts

Chickpea curry is a classic and flavorful dish, full of protein and bold spices, perfect for a spicy and satisfying meal.

4
servings

340

45

Vegan Stuffed Bell Peppers

Ingredients:

- 4 bell peppers, tops removed and seeds removed
- 1 cup quinoa
- 2 cups vegetable broth
- 1 cup black beans, drained and rinsed
- 1 cup corn kernels
- 1 cup tomatoes, diced
- 1/4 cup onions, chopped
- 1 tsp chili powder
- 1/2 tsp cumin
- 1/4 cup fresh cilantro, chopped
- Salt and pepper to taste
- 2 tbsp olive oil

Fun Facts

Stuffed bell peppers provide a colorful and nutritious meal with a hearty quinoa and veggie filling, perfect for a satisfying plant-based dish.

A colorful and vegan Stuffed Bell Peppers with a hearty quinoa and veggie filling, perfect for a nutritious and wholesome plant-based meal.

Directions

1. Preheat the oven to 375°F (190°C).
2. In a large pot, combine quinoa and vegetable broth. Bring to a boil, then reduce heat and simmer for 15-20 minutes until quinoa is cooked.
3. In a skillet, heat olive oil over medium heat. Add onions and sauté until soft.
4. Stir in black beans, corn, tomatoes, and all the spices. Cook for another 5 minutes.
5. Combine the cooked quinoa with the vegetable mixture. Season with salt and pepper.
6. Stuff the bell peppers with the quinoa filling.
7. Place the stuffed peppers in a baking dish and cover with foil.
8. Bake for 25-30 minutes until peppers are tender.

4 servings

380

40

Vegan Mushroom Risotto

Ingredients:

- 1 1/2 cups Arborio rice
- 8 cups vegetable broth
- 1 cup mixed mushrooms (e.g., cremini, shiitake), sliced
- 1/2 cup onions, chopped
- 2 cloves garlic, minced
- 1/4 cup white wine (optional)
- 2 tbsp olive oil
- 1/4 cup nutritional yeast
- 2 tbsp fresh thyme, chopped
- Salt and pepper to taste

Fun Facts

Mushroom risotto offers a creamy and comforting dish with a medley of savory mushrooms, perfect for a satisfying plant-based meal.

A creamy and vegan Mushroom Risotto with Arborio rice and a medley of mushrooms, perfect for a comforting and flavorful plant-based dish.

Directions

1. In a large pot, heat vegetable broth and keep it warm.
2. In a large skillet, heat olive oil over medium heat. Add onions and garlic, and sauté until soft.
3. Stir in Arborio rice and cook for 2 minutes.
4. If using white wine, add it and cook until absorbed.
5. Gradually add warm vegetable broth, one ladle at a time, stirring constantly until absorbed. Continue until the rice is creamy and tender.
6. In another skillet, sauté mushrooms until golden.
7. Stir in nutritional yeast and thyme.
8. Season with salt and pepper.
9. Fold the mushroom mixture into the risotto.

4
servings

360

30

Vegan Spinach and Chickpea Curry

Ingredients:

- 2 cans (15 oz each) chickpeas, drained
- 1 cup onions, chopped
- 2 cloves garlic, minced
- 1 tbsp ginger, minced
- 1 cup spinach, chopped
- 1 can (14 oz) diced tomatoes
- 1/4 cup tomato sauce
- 1 cup coconut milk
- 2 tbsp curry powder
- 1 tsp turmeric
- 1 tsp cumin
- Salt and pepper to taste
- 2 tbsp vegetable oil

A vibrant and vegan Spinach and Chickpea Curry with a rich and aromatic sauce, perfect for a nutritious and flavorful plant-based dish.

Directions

1. In a large skillet, heat vegetable oil over medium heat.
2. Add onions and sauté until soft.
3. Stir in garlic and ginger, and cook for another minute.
4. Add chickpeas, diced tomatoes, tomato sauce, coconut milk, and all the spices.
5. Simmer for 15-20 minutes until the sauce thickens.
6. Stir in chopped spinach and cook until wilted.
7. Season with salt and pepper.
8. Serve over rice or with naan bread.

Fun Facts

Spinach and chickpea curry offers a vibrant and nutritious dish with a rich and aromatic sauce, perfect for a satisfying plant-based meal.

4
servings

380

45

Vegan Eggplant Parmesan

A crispy and vegan Eggplant Parmesan with layers of eggplant, marinara sauce, and vegan cheese, perfect for a comforting and Italian-inspired dish.

Ingredients:

- 2 large eggplants, sliced
- 2 cups marinara sauce
- 1 1/2 cups vegan mozzarella cheese, shredded
- 1/2 cup vegan parmesan cheese
- 1/4 cup fresh basil leaves
- Salt and pepper to taste
- 2 tbsp olive oil

Directions

1. Preheat the oven to 375°F (190°C).
2. Lay out eggplant slices on a baking sheet. Sprinkle with salt and let them sit for 15 minutes.
3. Rinse the eggplant slices and pat dry.
4. In a large skillet, heat olive oil over medium heat. Add eggplant slices and cook until golden.
5. In a baking dish, layer marinara sauce, eggplant slices, vegan mozzarella cheese, vegan parmesan cheese, and fresh basil leaves.
6. Repeat the layers.
7. Bake for 30-35 minutes until bubbly and golden.

Fun Facts

Eggplant Parmesan offers a crispy and comforting dish with layers of eggplant and cheesy goodness, perfect for an Italian-inspired meal.

4 servings

360 kcal

50

Vegan Butternut Squash Lasagna

Ingredients:

- 1 butternut squash, peeled and sliced
- 1 cup spinach, chopped
- 1 1/2 cups vegan ricotta cheese
- 1/2 cup vegan mozzarella cheese, shredded
- 1/4 cup vegan parmesan cheese
- 1/4 cup fresh sage leaves
- 8 lasagna noodles
- Salt and pepper to taste
- 2 tbsp olive oil

Fun Facts

Butternut squash lasagna offers a creamy and hearty dish with layers of roasted squash and cheesy goodness, perfect for a satisfying plant-based meal.

A creamy and vegan Butternut Squash Lasagna with layers of roasted butternut squash, spinach, and vegan ricotta, perfect for a hearty and wholesome dish.

Directions

1. Preheat the oven to 375°F (190°C).
2. Lay out butternut squash slices on a baking sheet. Drizzle with olive oil and sprinkle with salt and pepper. Roast for 25-30 minutes until tender.
3. Cook lasagna noodles according to package instructions.
4. In a bowl, combine vegan ricotta, vegan mozzarella, and vegan parmesan cheese. Season with salt and pepper.
5. In a baking dish, layer roasted butternut squash, cooked lasagna noodles, spinach, sage leaves, and the cheese mixture.
6. Repeat the layers.
7. Bake for 30-35 minutes until bubbly and golden.

4 servings

340

40

Vegan Black Bean Enchiladas

A zesty and vegan Black Bean Enchiladas with a spicy red enchilada sauce, perfect for a flavorful and protein-packed plant-based dish.

Ingredients:

- 2 cans (15 oz each) black beans, drained
- 1 cup onions, chopped
- 2 cloves garlic, minced
- 1 tbsp chili powder
- 1 tsp cumin
- 1/2 tsp paprika
- 1 cup corn kernels
- 1/4 cup fresh cilantro, chopped
- 2 cups red enchilada sauce
- 1 cup vegan cheddar cheese, shredded
- 8 small tortillas
- Salt and pepper to taste
- 2 tbsp vegetable oil

Directions

1. In a large skillet, heat vegetable oil over medium heat.
2. Add onions and garlic, and sauté until soft.
3. Stir in chili powder, cumin, and paprika.
4. Add black beans, corn, and fresh cilantro. Cook for 5 minutes.
5. Preheat the oven to 375°F (190°C).
6. In a baking dish, spread a bit of enchilada sauce.
7. Fill each tortilla with the black bean mixture and roll it up. Place it in the baking dish.
8. Pour the remaining enchilada sauce over the top.
9. Sprinkle with vegan cheddar cheese.
10. Bake for 20-25 minutes until bubbly and golden.

Fun Facts

Black bean enchiladas offer a zesty and protein-packed dish with a spicy red sauce, perfect for a flavorful plant-based meal.

4
servings

360

30

Vegan Cauliflower Steak

Ingredients:

- 1 large cauliflower head
- 1/4 cup olive oil
- 1 tsp smoked paprika
- 1 tsp garlic powder
- 1/2 tsp cumin
- Salt and pepper to taste
- 1/4 cup fresh parsley, chopped

A hearty and vegan Cauliflower Steak with a smoky paprika sauce, perfect for a savory and satisfying plant-based dish.

Directions

1. Preheat the oven to 425°F (220°C).
2. Remove the leaves from the cauliflower head, but keep it whole.
3. In a small bowl, mix olive oil, smoked paprika, garlic powder, cumin, salt, and pepper.
4. Brush the cauliflower with the paprika mixture.
5. Roast for 30-35 minutes until tender and golden.
6. Sprinkle with fresh parsley before serving.

Fun Facts

Cauliflower steak offers a hearty and smoky dish with a delicious paprika sauce, perfect for a satisfying and savory plant-based meal.

4
servings

340

40

Vegan Sweet Potato Gnocchi

Ingredients:

- 2 large sweet potatoes
- 2 cups all-purpose flour
- 1/4 cup vegan butter
- 1/4 cup fresh sage leaves
- Salt and pepper to taste
- 1/4 cup vegan parmesan cheese

Fun Facts

Sweet potato gnocchi offers a pillowy and comforting dish with a fragrant sage-infused brown butter sauce, perfect for an Italian-inspired plant-based meal.

A pillowy and vegan Sweet Potato Gnocchi with a sage-infused brown butter sauce, perfect for a comforting and Italian-inspired plant-based dish.

Directions

1. Preheat the oven to 400°F (200°C).
2. Roast sweet potatoes for 45-50 minutes until tender.
3. Let them cool, then scoop out the flesh and mash it.
4. In a large bowl, combine mashed sweet potatoes with flour, salt, and pepper. Knead into a smooth dough.
5. Roll the dough into long ropes and cut into bite-sized pieces.
6. In a pot, bring salted water to a boil. Cook gnocchi until they float to the surface.
7. In a skillet, heat vegan butter over medium heat. Add sage leaves and cook until fragrant.
8. Toss cooked gnocchi in the brown butter sauce.
9. Sprinkle with vegan parmesan before serving.

Chapter 9:
Easy Sides and Snacks

4
servings

180

30

Vegan Roasted Brussels Sprouts

Ingredients:

- 1 lb Brussels sprouts, trimmed and halved
- 2 tbsp olive oil
- 2 tbsp balsamic vinegar
- 1 tsp smoked paprika
- Salt and pepper to taste
- 1/4 cup vegan parmesan cheese (optional)

A crispy and vegan Roasted Brussels Sprouts with a smoky balsamic glaze, perfect for a flavorful side.

Directions

1. Preheat the oven to 400°F (200°C).
2. In a bowl, toss Brussels sprouts with olive oil, balsamic vinegar, smoked paprika, salt, and pepper.
3. Spread them on a baking sheet.
4. Roast for 25-30 minutes until crispy and caramelized.
5. Sprinkle with vegan parmesan before serving.

Fun Facts

Roasted Brussels sprouts offer a crispy and flavorful side with a smoky balsamic glaze, perfect for any meal.

4
servings

320

20

Vegan Garlic Bread

Ingredients:

- 1 baguette or Italian bread
- 1/2 cup vegan butter, softened
- 4 cloves garlic, minced
- 2 tbsp fresh parsley, chopped
- Salt to taste

A classic and vegan Garlic Bread with a fragrant garlic and herb butter, perfect for a tasty and comforting snack.

Directions

1. Preheat the oven to 350°F (175°C).
2. Slice the bread in half lengthwise.
3. In a bowl, combine vegan butter, minced garlic, chopped parsley, and a pinch of salt.
4. Spread the garlic butter mixture over the bread halves.
5. Wrap the bread in aluminum foil.
6. Bake for 10-15 minutes until the butter is melted and the bread is crispy.

Fun Facts

Garlic bread offers a classic and comforting snack with fragrant garlic and herb butter, perfect for sharing.

4
servings

160

30

Vegan Roasted Cauliflower

Ingredients:

- 1 head cauliflower, cut into florets
- 2 tbsp olive oil
- Salt and pepper to taste
- Optional seasonings: paprika, cumin, turmeric, garlic powder, etc.

Fun Facts

Roasted cauliflower offers a simple and versatile side dish that pairs well with various seasonings, perfect for any meal.

A simple and vegan Roasted Cauliflower with olive oil and your choice of seasonings, perfect for an easy and versatile side.

Directions

1. Preheat the oven to 425°F (220°C).
2. In a bowl, toss cauliflower florets with olive oil, salt, pepper, and your choice of seasonings.
3. Spread them on a baking sheet.
4. Roast for 25-30 minutes until tender and slightly crispy.

4
servings

240

40

Vegan Zucchini Fritters

Ingredients:

- 2 medium zucchinis, grated and squeezed to remove excess liquid
- 1/4 cup all-purpose flour
- 1/4 cup fresh herbs (e.g., dill, parsley), chopped
- 2 cloves garlic, minced
- 1/4 cup vegan feta cheese, crumbled
- Salt and pepper to taste
- 2 tbsp vegetable oil

Crispy and vegan Zucchini Fritters with fresh herbs and a zesty dipping sauce, perfect for a delightful and savory snack.

Directions

1. In a bowl, combine grated zucchini, all-purpose flour, fresh herbs, minced garlic, crumbled vegan feta cheese, salt, and pepper.
2. Heat vegetable oil in a skillet over medium heat.
3. Form the zucchini mixture into small patties and place them in the skillet.
4. Cook until golden and crispy, about 3-4 minutes per side.
5. Serve with your favorite dipping sauce.

Fun Facts

Zucchini fritters offer a crispy and savory snack with fresh herbs and zesty vegan feta, perfect for a delightful appetizer.

4
servings

220

30

Vegan Stuffed Mushrooms

Ingredients:

- 12 large button mushrooms
- 1/2 cup breadcrumbs
- 2 cloves garlic, minced
- 2 tbsp fresh parsley, chopped
- 2 tbsp vegan cream cheese
- 2 tbsp vegan parmesan cheese
- Salt and pepper to taste
- 2 tbsp olive oil

A delightful and vegan Stuffed Mushrooms with a savory breadcrumb and herb filling, perfect for an elegant appetizer.

Directions

1. Preheat the oven to 375°F (190°C).
2. Remove the stems from the mushrooms and set them aside.
3. In a bowl, combine breadcrumbs, minced garlic, chopped parsley, vegan cream cheese, vegan parmesan, salt, and pepper.
4. Stuff each mushroom with the breadcrumb mixture.
5. Drizzle with olive oil.
6. Bake for 20-25 minutes until mushrooms are tender and the filling is golden.

Fun Facts

Stuffed mushrooms offer a delightful and elegant appetizer with a savory breadcrumb and herb filling, perfect for any gathering.

4
servings

180

15

Vegan Guacamole

A classic and vegan Guacamole with ripe avocados, fresh lime, and a burst of flavors, perfect for a zesty dip.

Ingredients:

- 3 ripe avocados, peeled and mashed
- 1/2 cup red onion, finely chopped
- 2 cloves garlic, minced
- 1-2 tomatoes, diced
- 1/4 cup fresh cilantro, chopped
- Juice of 1-2 limes
- Salt and pepper to taste
- 1-2 jalapeño peppers, finely chopped (adjust to taste)

Directions

1. In a bowl, combine mashed avocados, chopped red onion, minced garlic, diced tomatoes, chopped cilantro, and the juice of 1-2 limes.
2. Season with salt, pepper, and chopped jalapeño peppers to taste.
3. Mix well and serve with tortilla chips or as a topping.

Fun Facts

Guacamole offers a classic and zesty dip with ripe avocados and fresh lime, perfect for a burst of flavors at any gathering.

4
servings

160

30

Vegan Roasted Carrot Fries

Crispy and vegan Roasted Carrot Fries with a sprinkle of fresh herbs, perfect for a nutritious and colorful side.

Ingredients:

- 1 lb carrots, peeled and cut into fries- 2 tbsp olive oil- 2 tsp fresh thyme, chopped- 1 tsp fresh rosemary, chopped- Salt and pepper to taste

Directions

1. Preheat the oven to 425°F (220°C).
2. In a bowl, toss carrot fries with olive oil, fresh thyme, fresh rosemary, salt, and pepper.
3. Spread them on a baking sheet.
4. Roast for 25-30 minutes until crispy and slightly caramelized.

Fun Facts

Carrot fries offer a crispy and colorful side with a hint of fresh herbs, perfect for a nutritious addition to any meal.

4
servings

200

40

Vegan Buffalo Cauliflower Bites

Spicy and vegan Buffalo Cauliflower Bites with a tangy buffalo sauce, perfect for a fiery and addictive snack.

Ingredients:

- 1 head cauliflower, cut into florets
- 1/2 cup all-purpose flour
- 1/2 cup water
- 1 tsp garlic powder
- 1 tsp onion powder
- 1/4 cup hot sauce
- 2 tbsp vegan butter, melted
- Salt and pepper to taste
- 1-2 green onions, chopped (optional)

Directions

1. Preheat the oven to 450°F (230°C).
2. In a bowl, whisk together all-purpose flour, water, garlic powder, and onion powder.
3. Dip cauliflower florets into the batter, letting excess drip off.
4. Place them on a baking sheet and roast for 20-25 minutes until crispy.
5. In a bowl, combine hot sauce and melted vegan butter.
6. Toss the roasted cauliflower in the buffalo sauce.
7. Season with salt and pepper.
8. Sprinkle with chopped green onions before serving.

Fun Facts

Buffalo cauliflower bites offer a spicy and addictive snack with a tangy buffalo sauce, perfect for a fiery appetizer.

4
servings

260

35

Vegan Spinach and Artichoke Dip

A creamy and vegan Spinach and Artichoke Dip with a hint of garlic and melty vegan cheese, perfect for a comforting dip.

Ingredients:

- 1 cup frozen chopped spinach, thawed and squeezed dry
- 1 can (14 oz) artichoke hearts, drained and chopped
- 1/2 cup vegan cream cheese
- 1/2 cup vegan mayonnaise
- 1/2 cup vegan mozzarella cheese, shredded
- 2 cloves garlic, minced
- Salt and pepper to taste
- 1/4 cup vegan parmesan cheese

Directions

1. Preheat the oven to 375°F (190°C).
2. In a bowl, combine thawed spinach, chopped artichoke hearts, vegan cream cheese, vegan mayonnaise, vegan mozzarella, minced garlic, salt, and pepper.
3. Transfer the mixture to a baking dish.
4. Sprinkle with vegan parmesan cheese.
5. Bake for 25-30 minutes until bubbly and golden.

Fun Facts

Spinach and artichoke dip offers a creamy and comforting dip with a hint of garlic and melty vegan cheese, perfect for sharing.

4
servings

200

10

Vegan Edamame

Ingredients:

- 2 cups frozen edamame, in the pod
- Sea salt to taste

A simple and vegan Edamame with a sprinkle of sea salt, perfect for a quick and protein-packed snack.

Directions

1. Bring a pot of salted water to a boil.
2. Add edamame and cook for 5-7 minutes until tender.
3. Drain and sprinkle with sea salt.

Fun Facts

Edamame offers a simple and protein-packed snack, perfect for a quick and nutritious treat.

Chapter 10:
Sweet and Simple Desserts

4
servings

250

15

Vegan Chocolate Avocado Mousse

Ingredients:

- 2 ripe avocados, peeled and pitted
- 1/2 cup unsweetened cocoa powder
- 1/4 cup maple syrup
- 1/4 cup coconut milk
- 1 tsp vanilla extract
- A pinch of salt
- Fresh berries for garnish (optional)

A velvety and vegan Chocolate Avocado Mousse with a rich and creamy texture, perfect for a guilt-free dessert.

Directions

1. In a food processor, combine ripe avocados, unsweetened cocoa powder, maple syrup, coconut milk, vanilla extract, and a pinch of salt.
2. Blend until smooth and creamy.
3. Divide the mousse into serving glasses.
4. Chill in the refrigerator for at least 30 minutes.
5. Garnish with fresh berries before serving, if desired.

Fun Facts

Chocolate avocado mousse offers a guilt-free and velvety dessert with a rich and creamy texture, perfect for chocolate lovers.

4
servings

160

10

Vegan Banana Nice Cream

A simple and vegan Banana Nice Cream with frozen bananas, perfect for a naturally sweet and refreshing dessert.

Ingredients:

- 4 ripe bananas, peeled, sliced, and frozen
- 1 tsp vanilla extract
- Toppings of your choice: nuts, berries, chocolate chips, etc.

Directions

1. In a food processor, combine frozen banana slices and vanilla extract.
2. Blend until smooth and creamy, scraping down the sides as needed.
3. Serve immediately as a soft-serve ice cream or freeze for a firmer texture.
4. Top with your favorite toppings.

Fun Facts

Banana nice cream offers a naturally sweet and refreshing dessert made with frozen bananas, perfect for a guilt-free treat.

4
servings

220

20

Vegan Peanut Butter Cookies

Ingredients:

- 1 cup peanut butter
- 1/2 cup brown sugar
- 1 flax egg (1 tbsp ground flaxseed + 3 tbsp water)
- 1 tsp vanilla extract
- A pinch of salt
- 1/2 tsp baking soda

Fun Facts

Peanut butter cookies offer a classic and comforting sweet treat with a delightful peanut flavor, perfect for any occasion.

A classic and vegan Peanut Butter Cookies with a delightful peanut flavor, perfect for a comforting sweet treat.

Directions

1. Preheat the oven to 350°F (175°C).
2. In a bowl, combine peanut butter, brown sugar, flax egg, vanilla extract, salt, and baking soda.
3. Mix until the dough comes together.
4. Roll the dough into balls and place them on a baking sheet.
5. Flatten each cookie with a fork, making a crisscross pattern.
6. Bake for 10-12 minutes until golden.
7. Let cool on a wire rack.

4
servings

180

15

Vegan Berry Parfait

A delightful and vegan Berry Parfait with layers of fresh berries and creamy coconut yogurt, perfect for a refreshing dessert.

Ingredients:

- 2 cups mixed berries (e.g., strawberries, blueberries, raspberries)
- 2 cups coconut yogurt
- 2 tbsp maple syrup (optional)
- Granola for topping (optional)

Directions

1. In serving glasses, layer coconut yogurt, mixed berries, and a drizzle of maple syrup if desired.
2. Repeat the layers.
3. Top with granola for a crunchy texture, if desired.
4. Serve immediately.

Fun Facts

Berry parfait offers a delightful and refreshing dessert with fresh berries and creamy coconut yogurt, perfect for a light and fruity treat.

4
servings

280

35

Vegan Apple Crisp

Ingredients:

- 4 apples, peeled, cored, and sliced
- 1 tbsp lemon juice
- 1/2 cup rolled oats
- 1/4 cup flour
- 1/4 cup brown sugar
- 1/4 cup vegan butter, softened
- 1 tsp cinnamon
- A pinch of salt

Fun Facts

Apple crisp offers a warm and comforting dessert with crispy oat topping and cinnamon-spiced apples, perfect for a cozy treat.

A warm and vegan Apple Crisp with a crispy oat topping, perfect for a comforting and cinnamon-spiced dessert.

Directions

1. Preheat the oven to 350°F (175°C).
2. In a bowl, toss apple slices with lemon juice.
3. In another bowl, combine rolled oats, flour, brown sugar, softened vegan butter, cinnamon, and a pinch of salt.
4. Place the apples in a baking dish and sprinkle the oat mixture on top.
5. Bake for 25-30 minutes until the topping is crispy and apples are tender.
6. Serve warm with vegan ice cream or whipped coconut cream, if desired.

4
servings

200

20

Vegan Coconut Bliss Balls

Ingredients:

- 1 cup mixed nuts (e.g., almonds, cashews, walnuts)
- 1 cup pitted dates
- 1/2 cup shredded coconut
- 1-2 tbsp cocoa powder (optional)
- 1 tsp vanilla extract (optional)
- A pinch of salt

A wholesome and vegan Coconut Bliss Balls with a mix of nuts, dates, and coconut, perfect for a quick and nutritious snack.

Directions

1. In a food processor, combine mixed nuts, pitted dates, shredded coconut, cocoa powder, vanilla extract, and a pinch of salt.
2. Blend until the mixture is sticky and holds together.
3. Roll the mixture into small balls.
4. Refrigerate for 30 minutes to firm up.
5. Store in an airtight container.

Fun Facts

Coconut bliss balls offer a wholesome and nutritious snack with a mix of nuts, dates, and coconut, perfect for an energy boost.

4
servings

150

20

Vegan Chocolate-Dipped Strawberries

Ingredients:

- 1 pint fresh strawberries, rinsed and dried
- 4 oz vegan dark chocolate, melted

A romantic and vegan Chocolate-Dipped Strawberries with luscious dark chocolate, perfect for a sweet and elegant dessert.

Directions

1. Line a baking sheet with parchment paper.
2. Dip each strawberry into the melted dark chocolate, allowing excess to drip off.
3. Place the dipped strawberries on the prepared baking sheet.
4. Refrigerate for 10-15 minutes until the chocolate is set.

Fun Facts

Chocolate-dipped strawberries offer a romantic and elegant dessert with luscious dark chocolate, perfect for special occasions.

4
servings

180

20

Vegan Rice Krispie Treats

Ingredients:

- 4 cups crispy rice cereal
- 1/4 cup vegan butter
- 1 package (10 oz) vegan marshmallows
- A pinch of salt

A childhood favorite, vegan Rice Krispie Treats made with vegan marshmallows and crispy rice cereal, perfect for a nostalgic sweet snack.

Directions

1. In a large saucepan, melt vegan butter over low heat.
2. Add vegan marshmallows and a pinch of salt. Stir until completely melted and smooth.
3. Remove from heat.
4. Quickly fold in the crispy rice cereal and mix until well coated.
5. Press the mixture into a greased 8x8-inch pan.
6. Let cool and set before cutting into squares.

Fun Facts

Rice Krispie treats offer a childhood favorite made with vegan marshmallows and crispy rice cereal, perfect for a sweet and nostalgic snack.

4
servings

220

35

Vegan Lemon Bars

A tangy and vegan Lemon Bars with a zesty lemon filling and a buttery shortbread crust, perfect for a citrusy and sweet dessert.

Ingredients:

- For the crust:
 - 1 cup all-purpose flour
- 1/2 cup vegan butter, softened
- 1/4 cup powdered sugar
- For the lemon filling:
 - 1 cup granulated sugar
- 2 tbsp all-purpose flour
- 1/2 tsp baking powder
- 1/4 cup fresh lemon juice
- 2 tsp lemon zest
- 2 flax eggs (2 tbsp ground flaxseed + 6 tbsp water)
- Powdered sugar for dusting

Directions

For the crust:
1. Preheat the oven to 350°F (175°C).
2. In a bowl, combine all-purpose flour, softened vegan butter, and powdered sugar.
3. Press the mixture into a greased 8x8-inch pan.
4. Bake for 20-25 minutes until lightly golden.
5. For the lemon filling:
6. In a separate bowl, combine granulated sugar, all-purpose flour, baking powder, fresh lemon juice, lemon zest, and flax eggs.
7. Pour the lemon filling over the baked crust.
8. Bake for an additional 20-25 minutes until the filling is set.
9. Let cool, then dust with powdered sugar and cut into squares.

Fun Facts

Lemon bars offer a tangy and citrusy dessert with a zesty lemon filling and a buttery shortbread crust, perfect for a sweet indulgence.

4
servings

240

25

Vegan Oatmeal Raisin Cookies

A classic and vegan Oatmeal Raisin Cookies with a chewy texture and a hint of cinnamon, perfect for a comforting sweet treat.

Ingredients:

- 1 cup rolled oats
- 1 cup all-purpose flour
- 1/2 cup vegan butter, softened
- 1/2 cup brown sugar
- 1/4 cup granulated sugar
- 1 flax egg (1 tbsp ground flaxseed + 3 tbsp water)
- 1 tsp vanilla extract
- 1/2 tsp baking soda
- 1/2 tsp ground cinnamon
- 1/4 tsp salt
- 1/2 cup raisins

Directions

1. Preheat the oven to 350°F (175°C).
2. In a bowl, combine rolled oats, all-purpose flour, softened vegan butter, brown sugar, granulated sugar, flax egg, vanilla extract, baking soda, ground cinnamon, and salt.
3. Fold in the raisins.
4. Drop spoonfuls of cookie dough onto a baking sheet.
5. Bake for 10-12 minutes until golden.
6. Let cool on a wire rack.

Fun Facts

Oatmeal raisin cookies offer a classic and comforting sweet treat with a chewy texture and a hint of cinnamon, perfect for any occasion.

Chapter 11:
Plant-Based Beverages

2
servings

150

10

Vegan Green Smoothie

Ingredients:

- 2 cups fresh spinach leaves
- 2 ripe bananas
- 1 cup unsweetened almond milk
- 1/2 cup fresh pineapple chunks
- 1 tbsp chia seeds (optional)
- 1 tsp honey or maple syrup (optional)

A nutritious and refreshing Vegan Green Smoothie with spinach, banana, and a burst of green goodness, perfect for a healthful start.

Directions

1. In a blender, combine fresh spinach leaves, ripe bananas, unsweetened almond milk, fresh pineapple chunks, chia seeds, and honey or maple syrup if desired.
2. Blend until smooth and creamy.
3. Serve immediately.

Fun Facts

Green smoothie offers a nutritious and refreshing start to the day with spinach, banana, and a burst of green goodness.

4
servings

40

15

Vegan Almond Milk

Ingredients:

- 1 cup raw almonds, soaked and drained
- 4 cups water
- Sweetener of your choice: dates, maple syrup, agave syrup, etc. (optional)
- 1 tsp vanilla extract (optional)
- A pinch of salt

Fun Facts

Homemade almond milk offers a creamy and dairy-free alternative to store-bought options, perfect for various recipes.

A simple and vegan Almond Milk made from scratch, perfect for a creamy and dairy-free alternative.

Directions

1. In a blender, combine soaked and drained raw almonds, water, sweetener of your choice, vanilla extract, and a pinch of salt if desired.
2. Blend until smooth.
3. Strain the mixture through a nut milk bag or fine mesh strainer.
4. Store in the refrigerator for up to 3-4 days.

2
servings

100

10

Vegan Chai Latte

Ingredients:

- 2 cups unsweetened plant-based milk (e.g., almond, soy, oat)
- 2 chai tea bags or 2 tbsp loose -leaf chai tea
- Sweetener of your choice: maple syrup, honey, agave syrup, etc.
- Ground cinnamon and nutmeg for garnish (optional)

Fun Facts

Chai latte offers a cozy and aromatic beverage with a blend of spices and plant-based milk, perfect for a warm indulgence.

A cozy and vegan Chai Latte with a blend of spices and plant-based milk, perfect for a warm and aromatic beverage.

Directions

1. In a saucepan, heat unsweetened plant-based milk with chai tea bags or loose-leaf chai tea.
2. Simmer for 5-7 minutes, or until the desired chai flavor is achieved.
3. Sweeten with your choice of sweetener.
4. Remove the tea bags or strain the loose-leaf tea.
5. Pour into mugs and garnish with ground cinnamon and nutmeg if desired.

2
servings

90

10

Vegan Matcha Latte

Ingredients:

- 2 tsp matcha green tea powder
- 2 cups unsweetened plant-based milk (e.g., almond, soy, oat)
- Sweetener of your choice: maple syrup, agave syrup, etc. (optional)
- Hot water for whisking
- Ground matcha for garnish (optional)

Fun Facts

Matcha latte offers a vibrant and antioxidant-rich drink with green tea powder and frothy plant-based milk, perfect for a refreshing beverage.

A vibrant and vegan Matcha Latte with green tea powder and frothy plant-based milk, perfect for a vibrant and antioxidant-rich drink.

Directions

1. In a small bowl, whisk matcha green tea powder with a small amount of hot water until smooth.
2. In a saucepan, heat unsweetened plant-based milk.
3. Whisk in the matcha mixture and sweetener of your choice.
4. Whisk until frothy.
5. Pour into mugs and garnish with ground matcha if desired.

2
servings

160

10

Vegan Strawberry Banana Smoothie

A fruity and vegan Strawberry Banana Smoothie with ripe strawberries, banana, and a touch of sweetness, perfect for a fruity delight.

Ingredients:

- 2 cups ripe strawberries
- 2 ripe bananas
- 1 cup unsweetened almond milk
- 1/2 cup dairy-free yogurt
- 1-2 tbsp honey or maple syrup (optional)

Directions

1. In a blender, combine ripe strawberries, ripe bananas, unsweetened almond milk, dairy-free yogurt, and honey or maple syrup if desired.
2. Blend until smooth and creamy.
3. Serve immediately.

Fun Facts

Strawberry banana smoothie offers a fruity and delightful drink with ripe strawberries, banana, and a touch of sweetness, perfect for a refreshing treat.

2
servings

90

10

Vegan Golden Milk

A soothing and vegan Golden Milk with turmeric, ginger, and plant-based milk, perfect for a warm and anti-inflammatory beverage.

Ingredients:

- 2 cups unsweetened plant-based milk (e.g., almond, coconut)
- 1 tsp ground turmeric
- 1/2 tsp ground ginger
- A pinch of black pepper
- Sweetener of your choice: honey, maple syrup, etc. (optional)

Directions

1. In a saucepan, heat unsweetened plant-based milk with ground turmeric, ground ginger, a pinch of black pepper, and your choice of sweetener.
2. Simmer for 5-7 minutes, stirring frequently.
3. Pour into mugs and serve warm.

Fun Facts

Golden milk offers a soothing and anti-inflammatory beverage with turmeric, ginger, and plant-based milk, perfect for a cozy and warming drink.

2
servings

180

10

Vegan Blueberry Protein Shake

A protein-packed and vegan Blueberry Protein Shake with blueberries, plant-based protein, and almond milk, perfect for a nutritious boost.

Ingredients:

- 2 cups frozen blueberries
- 2 scoops plant-based protein powder (e.g., pea, hemp)
- 2 cups unsweetened almond milk
- 1-2 tbsp honey or maple syrup (optional)
- Fresh blueberries for garnish (optional)

Directions

1. In a blender, combine frozen blueberries, plant-based protein powder, unsweetened almond milk, and honey or maple syrup if desired.
2. Blend until smooth and creamy.
3. Pour into glasses and garnish with fresh blueberries if desired.

Fun Facts

Blueberry protein shake offers a protein-packed and nutritious boost with blueberries, plant-based protein, and almond milk, perfect for a satisfying drink.

2
servings

80

10

Vegan
Watermelon
Cucumber Cooler

Ingredients:

- 2 cups fresh watermelon chunks
- 1/2 cucumber, peeled and sliced
- 1/4 cup fresh mint leaves
- 1 lime, juiced
- 1-2 tbsp honey or agave syrup (optional)
- Ice cubes for serving (optional)

A hydrating and vegan Watermelon Cucumber Cooler with a refreshing blend of watermelon, cucumber, and mint, perfect for a cooling summer beverage.

Directions

1. In a blender, combine fresh watermelon chunks, peeled and sliced cucumber, fresh mint leaves, lime juice, and honey or agave syrup if desired.
2. Blend until smooth.
3. Strain the mixture to remove any solids.
4. Serve over ice if desired.

Fun Facts

Watermelon cucumber cooler offers a hydrating and refreshing summer beverage with watermelon, cucumber, and mint, perfect for staying cool.

2
servings

60

5

Vegan Iced Coffee

A chilled and vegan Iced Coffee with a strong brew and your choice of plant-based milk, perfect for a caffeine boost on a hot day.

Ingredients:

- 2 cups strong brewed coffee, cooled
- 1-2 cups unsweetened plant-based milk (e.g., almond, soy)
- Sweetener of your choice: sugar, syrup, etc. (optional)
- Ice cubes for serving (optional)

Directions

1. In a pitcher, combine strong brewed coffee and your choice of unsweetened plant-based milk.
2. Sweeten with your choice of sweetener, if desired.
3. Serve over ice if you prefer iced coffee.

Fun Facts

Iced coffee offers a chilled and caffeinated beverage with a strong brew and your choice of plant-based milk, perfect for a refreshing pick-me-up.

2
servings

220

10

Vegan Chocolate Protein Shake

Ingredients:

- 2 cups unsweetened almond milk
- 2 scoops plant-based chocolate protein powder
- 2 tbsp unsweetened cocoa powder
- 1-2 tbsp honey or maple syrup (optional)
- Ice cubes for serving (optional)

A protein-rich and vegan Chocolate Protein Shake with cocoa, plant-based protein, and almond milk, perfect for a post-workout recovery.

Directions

1. In a blender, combine unsweetened almond milk, plant-based chocolate protein powder, unsweetened cocoa powder, and honey or maple syrup if desired.
2. Blend until smooth and creamy.
3. Serve with ice if desired.

Fun Facts

Chocolate protein shake offers a protein-rich and post-workout recovery drink with cocoa, plant-based protein, and almond milk, perfect for replenishing energy.

We have a small favor to ask

Dear Fantastic Fans of Plant-Based Cuisine,

We've embarked on an extraordinary journey of flavor and health together, exploring the world of "Plant-Based 5-Ingredient" cooking. Throughout this culinary adventure, we've discovered the immense joy in creating simple, wholesome, and mouthwatering plant-based dishes.

In these pages, we've strived to provide you with over 100 recipes that will not only tantalize your taste buds but also contribute to your well-being. Your journey towards a healthier you is a path we're honored to accompany you on.

Now, as our book concludes, we find ourselves at a crossroads, and we humbly seek your support. Reviews, dear friends, are the lifeblood of small publishers like us. Your star ratings, your brief comments, and a few lines of your thoughts mean the world to us. We genuinely appreciate each and every review, as it fuels our passion for plant-based cuisine and provides invaluable insight into your culinary desires.

If you could spare a moment, please revisit the platform or app where you acquired this book. Your review, your rating, and your feedback are instrumental in helping us reach a wider audience, sharing the wonders of plant-based cooking with even more food enthusiasts.

In the realm of cooking, we acknowledge that, much like the perfect vegan dish, the occasional hiccup might occur. We've dedicated ourselves to offering you a seamless experience, but sometimes, minor oversights may take place. We hope you can pardon any small hiccups and understand that they are part and parcel of the culinary world.

Looking ahead, we promise to continue crafting cookbooks that celebrate the art of plant-based cuisine. Your reviews will serve as our guiding stars, lighting the path to future plant-based creations.

In closing, we extend our deepest gratitude for taking this journey with us. Your plant-based meals have become a testament to the amazing possibilities of plant-based cooking, and your reviews have the power to ignite the same passion in others.

May your culinary adventures always be filled with the vibrant colors and flavors of plant-based cuisine, and may your reviews continue to inspire more to explore this enriching path.

With boundless appreciation,

Garden of Grapes